Nine American Women of the Nineteenth Century

In memory of my grandmother,
Rachel McKillip Bolton,
born in the nineteenth century,
but possessor of a twentieth-century outlook

Nine American Women
of the Nineteenth Century

Leaders into the Twentieth

by

Moira Davison Reynolds

McFarland & Company, Inc., Publishers
Jefferson, North Carolina, and London

Library of Congress Cataloguing-in-Publication Data

Reynolds, Moira Davison.
  Nine American women of the nineteenth century.

  Bibliography: p. 149.
  Includes index.
  1. Feminists — United States — Biography. 2. Women's
rights — United States — History — 19th century. 3. Women —
United States — Social conditions. I. Title. II. Title:
9 American women of the 19th century.
HQ1412.R49 1988   305.4′092′2   87–43169

ISBN 0–89950–325–X (55# acid-free natural paper)

Printed in the United States of America.

McFarland   Box 611   Jefferson NC 28640

Contents

Illustrations

Preface and Acknowledgments

This book is for the general reader who has a serious interest in American history, and it may have special appeal to women.

The subjects were picked according to these criteria: each woman must have been American; each must have contributed something enduring to the culture of this country; her significant work must have been accomplished during the nineteenth century. A number of women qualify, but I chose those who interested me most.

As in the past, Marquette's Peter White Public Library and Northern Michigan University's Lydia M. Olson Library have been my mainstays. A special thanks is due to Joanne Wilkins of Superiorland Library Cooperative for locating whatever I ordered through interlibrary loan.

I wish to acknowledge the assistance of Professors Earl Hilton and Richard Sonderegger, both of whom gave me valuable suggestions.

Finally, I am indebted to Mrs. Marijean McKelvy for very careful proofreading of the manuscript.

Moira Davison Reynolds
Marquette, Michigan

O beautiful for pilgrim feet,
Whose stern, impassioned stress
A thoroughfare for freedom beat
Across the wilderness!
—Katharine Lee Bates

Introduction

Higher education for women is so common today, we forget that it was once open only to men. The fight for equal education was begun in 1818 by Emma Willard, whose enduring monument is the Emma Willard School in Troy, New York.

Mary Lyon, another educator of the same period, provided strong support for Mrs. Willard's movement by opening in 1837 what is now Mount Holyoke College.

Americans of all walks of life use "Simon Legree" and "Uncle Tom" in conversation. They may or may not have read Harriet Beecher Stowe's famous work, written before the Civil War to show the evils of slavery, and still in print.

When that terrible war came, Julia Ward Howe composed a great religious poem, "Battle Hymn of the Republic." It remains a national treasure.

Little Women by Louisa May Alcott came out just after the war and remains in print. Millions of American women have read it, cried over it, and recommended it to their present-day daughters and granddaughters.

As European immigrants poured into the rapidly growing nation, Emma Lazarus wrote a sonnet that would give hope to the newcomers to these shores. Originally associated with the Statue of Liberty, the familiar part of this poem is now inscribed on marble at the International Arrival Building at Kennedy Airport.

With transcontinental railway routes reality, the native American was suffering more and more. To draw attention to injustices inflicted upon Indians, Helen Hunt Jackson wrote *Ramona,* a novel that has seen many editions.

Wars, hurricanes, floods, and the like continue to plague us, and we continue to call on the American Red Cross for disaster relief. This humanitarian organization is a memorial to its founder, Clara Barton, who brought supplies and then nursed, comforted and cooked for soldiers at Antietam.

"America the Beautiful," published on July 4, 1895, is familiar to almost every citizen of the United States. Katharine Lee Bates, who wrote the words, was a professor of English at Wellesley College. This surely would have pleased Emma Willard.

This book is about these nine women of the nineteenth century and their enduring monuments. We shall see what motivated these women; how they used their native abilities; and how chance favored them. In the light of present-day thinking, some of their viewponts may seem prejudiced, shortsighted or antifeminist, for like ourselves they had weaknesses as well as strengths. But collectively they beat a thoroughfare for freedom into the present century, each leaving her own enduring monument.

Emma Hart Willard
Emma Willard School

The year was 1819. A poised and attractive woman, then just 32, had come from Middlebury, Vermont, to New York state's capital in Albany to interest legislators in her Plan for the Improvement of Female Education. She read this Plan to the lawmakers, explaining that the education of women would require the aid of the state. "Male education flourishes," she said, "because, from the guardian care of legislatures, the presidencies and professorships of our colleges, are some of the highest objects to which the eye of ambition is directed."

But this was not so with female institutions, she told her listeners: ". . . legislatures, undervaluing the importance of women in society, neglect to provide for their education . . . ."

She declared that the prosperity of the nation will depend on the character of its citizens; this character will be formed by their mothers; "and it is through the mothers that the government can control the character of future citizens, to form them such as will ensure the country's prosperity."

She rebuked the legislators: "Why then have you neglected our education? Why have you looked with lethargic indifference, on circumstances ruinous to the formation of our characters, which you might have controlled?"

The woman with the plan to improve the education of her sex was born on February 23, 1787, in Berlin, Connecticut, the sixteenth child of Samuel Hart and his second wife, Lydia. Emma, as she was named, attended the district public school. She was a good student and her father encouraged her search for knowledge. A prosperous farmer, Hart had fought in the Revolution and later represented Berlin in the state General Assembly in nearby Hartford. He was self-educated and an independent thinker. Often he read aloud to his children such works as *Paradise Lost* and Gibbons' *History of Rome.* By the time Emma was 15 she had acquired most of the knowledge available through the public school. At 12 she taught herself some geometry, supposedly some astronomy at 14, and it was clear that she had a studious bent. So she spent two years at a private academy for girls in Worthington, less than a mile from her home.

In keeping with the standards of her day, Emma was now equipped to teach, and in 1804 became mistress of the district school in Kensington, which was in session during the summer months only. The next winter, a brother financed additional study at Hartford, and in 1806 she was back at the academy in Berlin, but now as a teacher.

From the beginning Emma's teaching was a marked success. After her first year in Berlin she had offers to teach at girls' schools located in Westfield, Massachusetts; Hudson, New York; and Middlebury, Vermont. She chose Westfield, remaining there a year and teaching under the direction of men.

Emma next accepted the headship of the female academy at Middlebury. Middlebury College, founded in 1800 and open only to men, was located here, and for her its presence "made me bitterly feel the disparity in educational facilities between the two sexes." Emma once again showed her gift for teaching and was accepted enthusiastically by the townspeople.

In 1809 she married a well-to-do physician named John Willard who was 28 years her senior. Having given up medicine for politics, he was Marshal of Vermont, appointed by Thomas Jefferson. Emma inherited four stepchildren, the eldest her own age. A son, John Hart Willard, was born in 1810. This was Emma's only child.

Here is a part of a letter written to her husband when she was a full-time wife:

> The winter-apples are gathered; the cider is made — twenty-three barrels; the potatoes are nearly all in; the buckwheat is gathered, but lies on the barn-floor unthreshed, which, by the way, places us in a predicament about the wheat; the cows and hogs have been fed according to your directions; the carrots and garden vegetables are out yet, but will be gathered immediately; no injury has been done to the farm by unruly cattle; Wilcox has let us have a quarter of beef.

Although occupied with family cares, she found time to read her husband's medical books. He, like her father, encouraged her intellectual development. A nephew of the doctor's resided with the Willards while attending Middlebury College, and Emma took great interest in this young man's education, reading some of his books also.

In 1812 the Vermont State Bank, of which Dr. Willard was a director, was robbed and the directors had to make up the losses. Because of her husband's financial reverses, Emma in 1814 opened a school for girls in the Willard home. (This building is now owned by Middlebury College and is located on its campus.) According to her, ". . . my leading motive was to relieve my husband's financial difficulties. I also had the further motive of keeping a better school than those around me . . . ."

4   *Emma Hart Willard*

During the five-year existence of the Middlebury female academy, Emma worked constantly to improve its educational offerings. She gradually introduced into the curriculum mathematics, philosophy, history, foreign languages and literature, setting a new standard in the education of women. Much of the material was new to her and had to be mastered quickly before she could impart it to others. She also experimented with teaching methods. To underscore the proficiency of her scholars, she held public examinations. For those who believed that the female mind was incapable of academic pursuits, this practice should have removed all doubts. At any rate, her methods must have been considered successful, for soon she had 70 pupils enrolled.

In addition to heavy teaching and administrative responsibilities, Emma managed to work up her Plan, noted previously. In this she was encouraged by her husband: "He entered into the full spirit of my views with a disinterested zeal for the sex that, as he believed, his own had injuriously neglected." Writing the project took more than two years; she reworked it several times, rejecting about three-quarters of the original material. She called for a state-supported boarding school with a library, laboratory and suitable teaching aids such as maps. The average time for the course would be three years, with a girl entering at 14. The institution would provide a uniform curriculum stressing religion and moral values. Science and literature would not be neglected; domestic arts would be studied systematically; the ornamental branches such as drawing, painting, elegant penmanship, music and grace of motion would be optional. A board of trustees would manage the establishment.

While the Plan was being formulated, Emma intended to "inform myself and increase my personal influence and fame as a teacher, calculating that in this way I might be sought for in other places, where influential men would carry my project before some legislature, for the sake of obtaining a good school."

Through her students from Waterford, New York, her Plan, written in her own longhand, was given in 1818 to New York's Governor De Witt Clinton, known to favor state-supported education. Clinton was favorably impressed, and so that Emma could present her Plan in person, the Willards went to Albany for a short time while the legislature was in session.

Despite the governor's strong support, the best the legislature did was grant a charter to the Waterford Academy for Young Ladies and add that academy to the list of boys' institutions designated to receive part of the state's literary fund. A recommendation to grant an endowment of $5000 for the school was defeated.

But Emma believed so strongly in her Plan as a useful model that when she returned to Middlebury, she had it printed by W. J. Copeland and saw to its wide circulation. It went to John Adams, Thomas Jefferson and President Monroe; it was read by a lawmaker from Georgia who recommended it to his legislature; it even went to Europe where George Combe, Scottish lawyer and phrenologist, published it in his *Phrenological Journal.*

Still hopeful, the young educator moved her Middlebury school to Waterford in 1819. The town had leased a large building to house her operation, but there were no funds from the state. She had 22 boarders and trained a few of her former Middlebury pupils as teachers. The next year, Governor Clinton again asked his legislature to support the venture and not be "deterred by commonplace ridicule from extending your munificence to this meritorious institution." But his plea was in vain. The Assembly rejected an appropriation of $2000 passed by the Senate. Also, the regents of the University of the State of New York refused to donate anything from the literary fund. Like her father, Emma was a strong advocate of state-aided education. Thus New York's failure to act was a severe blow to her.

A letter written in 1820 stated that the terms at Waterford Academy were $42 per quarter for board and tuition in all the branches except music and dancing. Emma noted that the pupils were expected to furnish certain necessities, including their own candlesticks. But the school needed more than tuition to keep it in good shape. By the spring of 1821 the Willards were ready to close it.

At that juncture the city of Troy came to the rescue. On March 26, 1821, Troy's Common Council voted to raise $4000 by special tax to purchase a building for a female academy. Emma again moved her school, this time to Troy, and the money was raised. The Council also appointed a board of trustees for the school. This body in turn appointed an advisory council, composed of women of some influence.

In the fall of 1821 the Troy school had 90 students enrolled, about a third of them from Troy. The building that was supplied, known as Moulton's Coffee House, had been renovated and furnished under Emma's direction. It was three stories high with a ballroom and 22 other rooms.

Except for Dr. Willard's death in 1825, there would now be smoother sailing for Emma during the next 13 years. As time went by she would realize many of her educational goals. She was able to improve her course offerings and continued her practice of conducting public examinations. In 1824 the male college now known as Rensselaer Polytechnic Institute opened in Troy. According to professor Amos Eaton, Emma studied with him "every branch he was capable of teaching." Due to his influence the Troy girls were given science courses more advanced than those at most men's colleges. In 1823, Amelia Lincoln, a favorite sister of Emma's, lost her husband. The next year, she came to Troy to teach, remaining there for nine years. Mrs. Lincoln was very much interested in botany as well as in geology and chemistry, and her ability influenced the development of science at Emma's school. Later (1847–59), a Miss Mary Hastings used the same science texts as Yale and taught chemistry by means of experiments.

A shortage of good texts was a problem, but Emma's inventiveness came to the fore in surmounting this obstacle. In Waterford she had carved cones and pyramids from potatoes and turnips for her solid geometry classes, and now she decided that if she needed a text, she would write it herself, explaining any of her original pedagogy. When a geography book was in progress, she was consulted by William C. Woodbridge, who was also authoring one. They collaborated to produce a highly successful work, published in 1822. The financial rewards added to the security of the school. Other texts by Emma include several histories and one on astronomy. Her *Temple of Time, or Chronographer of Universal History* (1844) was a chart depicting the history of the world designed to save time in teaching and learning. It won a gold medal at the 1851 World's Fair in London.

In 1825 Troy Female Academy was visited by Lafayette, still revered for his part in the American Revolution and a personal hero of Emma's. Such occasions gave the school excellent publicity. But even without such a momentous visit, Emma's seminary was becoming well known. Girls came not only from New York state and Vermont, but from distant Ohio and Southern states. Sometimes boarders from far away regions stayed all summer, continuing their studies during that period. The average age was 17 (sometimes older girls and young widows were enrolled). A system of student government was instituted and proven successful. There was religious instruction, of course, but is was non-sectarian. It has been noted that although Emma never studied psychology, she seemed to known instinctively how to deal with young women, both from the standpoint of interesting them in academics and in the matter of discipline. One graduate referred to her as "a mother to us all."

As the United States developed rapidly into an industrial nation with a growing population and the Pacific Ocean as its western boundary, Emma realized the urgency of providing increased numbers of teachers. The school's fees made it impossible for many aspiring young women to attend, but now she provided a way. She granted free tuition to suitable candidates who would contract to pay back the cost when they became teachers. She managed to produce 200 teachers before the first public normal school graduated its entering class. In 1844 she wrote to a friend:

> I was engaged in teaching 30 years, and I have had in my charge as nearly as I can calculate, 5000 pupils, of whom as many as one in ten . . . have been teachers; and of these teachers, I think more than half have been those whom I have educated without present pay—their bills to be refunded from their earnings.

One biographer has estimated that she waived fees amounting to about $75,000. Unfortunately, much of this was never repaid.

In 1830 Emma made an extended visit to France and a shorter one to England and Scotland. Lafayette had not forgotten her, and through him she was able to visit French schools for girls. She was also invited to the Court of Louis Philippe and allowed to attend sessions of the Chamber of Deputies. She engaged a French teacher for her school and brought back books and works of art. On the return voyage Emma wrote the words of the hymn "Rocked in the Cradle of the Deep." It was first set to music by the Dule of Choiseul; later a melody composed by Joseph P. Knight was used. The work remained popular for many years; in fact, a century later it appeared in the *Seth Parker Hymnal. Emma's Journal and Letters from France and Great Britain,* published in 1833, recounts the experiences of her first European trip.

Rocked in the Cradle of the Deep

Rocked in the cradle of the deep,
I lay me down in peace to sleep;
Secure I rest upon the wave,
For Thou, O Lord! hast power to save;
I know thou wouldst not slight my call,
For Thou dost mark the sparrow's fall;
And calm and peaceful in my sleep,
Rocked in the cradle of the deep.

And such the trust that still were mine,
Though stormy winds swept o'er the brine,
And though the tempest's fiery breath
Roused me from sleep to wreck and death,
In ocean's cave, still safe with Thee,
The germ of immortality;
And calm and peaceful is my sleep,
Rocked in the cradle of the deep.

1831.

Around this time, Emma became interested in the education of Greek women. Greece had recently won independence from Turkey, and the time seemed ripe to train women teachers. Emma was instrumental in raising $3000 to be used to start a training school in Athens.

The Erie Canal brought prosperity to Troy. By 1836 the Seminary had 100 boarding students and 200 day scholars. The first building had been enlarged and another added. There would be more expansions in the years to come, for by mid-century some considered Troy Female Seminary the foremost girls' school in existence.

An outsider observes public examinations
at
Troy Female Seminary

Among other distinguished visitors, during the last examination, the Rev. Messers. Cox and Hoby were present, one day. They availed themselves of the invitation of Mrs. Willard, and examined the classes in Mathematics and Philosophy for themselves. It is apparent that they had never before seen a young lady demonstrate a problem in Euclid, or heard an analysis of Stewart's Philosophy from other than masculine lips. They were minute and searching in their questions, but the pupils solved every problem, and answered every query, with readiness and promptitude.

Sarah J. Hale
American Ladies' Magazine
September 1833

Eighteen years after Emma had made her original request for state aid, the school finally received a small state allowance; a permanent endowment was not realized during her lifetime. In time, Margaret Olivia Slocum Sage would use the fortune she inherited from her husband, Russell Sage, to build a new campus for her alma mater, endow it, and change its name from Troy Female Seminary to Emma Willard School. The institution still exists as an independent girls' boarding and day college-preparatory school, enrolling more than 300 students.

Here is the reminiscence of John Lord, one of Emma Willard's biographers, who lectured at her school when he was a young teacher:

I remember full well the half turban and half cap which was so becoming to Mrs. Willard, the elegant black dress and laces which adorned the rather large figure, the gracious smile which softened the solemn austerity of executive habits and the egotistic pleasantries which made her natural and attractive, although subject to unfriendly criticism. Never was there a franker woman. Never did a woman seem to enjoy her labors and duties more than she.... She lived, as it appeared to me, in rather unusual style for a teacher, with horses and carriages, and an army of servants, with pictures in the parlors, and works of beauty and taste—souvenirs of her European travels.

He also wrote in his diary in 1836:

Observers would, perhaps, detect egotism, vanity, and love of admiration; and seeing these, would be inclined to ridicule or slander her. But gradually I forgot and lost sight of all these peculiarities, in the unequivocal exhibition of the kindest feelings, of firmness of purpose, strength of will, of generous impulses, and lofty ends of action....

Emma Hart Willard. Courtesy Emma Willard School.

John Willard, Emma's son, married Sarah Lucretia Hudson in 1834. Miss Hudson had been a student at the Seminary and became vice-principal at 21. After their marriage, John became business manager of the school, while his wife continued as vice-principal.

In 1838 Emma remarried, leaving the institution in the care of her son and daughter-in-law, whom she promoted to principal. She was astute enough to make a legal arrangement that protected the school and her possessions. In other words, her property did not come under the control of Dr. Christopher Yates, her second husband.

The marriage was not a success, and after just nine months Emma left Yates. She lived for some time in Berlin, her birthplace, residing with a sister. In 1843 the marriage was dissolved by the Connecticut Legislature, which granted Emma the right to use the name Emma Willard.

In the nineteenth century a woman rarely left her husband, no matter how serious the reason. If she did take such a step, she was open to censure. Emma described herself as a mariner who had escaped shipwreck, "thankful for what is saved—for life, reason, friends, and a thousand comforts with which kind Providence has surrounded me."

It was not long until she became aware of the work of Henry Barnard, the Secretary of Connecticut's first Board of Commissioners of Common Schools. He served for $3 a day and expenses from 1839 to 1842, when the Commission was abolished. Barnard was deeply committed to reform in the state's common schools. When Kensington, which is part of Berlin, voted Emma Superintendent of Common Schools for the following season, she mustered up some of her old energy. She found that often children as old as ten could not write, and she set about to remedy this. (There is evidence that many children at that time were taught to read but did not write. Perhaps this was because there was such importance attached to Bible reading.)

She emphasized reading with expression, rather than monotoning. She discouraged rote memorization, writing to Barnard that it was less important for students to learn a few facts from books than "to give them the power of using books to profit." She also recommended to the Secretary that each school have a clock, noting that "teachers on low wages cannot afford to buy watches. . . ." Emma organized the women of Kensington into a "Female Common School Association," and she spent much time instructing teachers. She even reintroduced her practice of conducting public examinations.

In 1844 Emma returned to Troy at the urging of her son. She was 57 and still vitally interested in all phases of education. The next year, the County Superintendents of Common Schools invited her to their convention in Syracuse. She accepted and addressed 60 of them privately rather than speaking at the convention, since this was considered unladylike. Her presentation was published, prompting an invitation to conduct institutes for teachers in southern New York state.

Accompanied by a former pupil and using her own carriage, Emma visited Binghamton, Rome and other towns. She covered many thousands of miles and taught or counseled at least 500 teachers. She underscored, as she had many other times, the importance of employing persons likely to stay in the profession, pointing out that progress was difficult when teachers could be expected to stay for only a few months, as most male teachers did. She was convinced that women teachers would remain for longer periods. (Marriage would claim many of them, of course, and it was most unusual for married women to work.) She also advocated better salaries for those in the profession.

In 1846 Emma, with a niece, journeyed through much of the South and what is now the Midwest, to speak for education. She used private carriage, stagecoach, packet and canalboat. Everywhere she found former pupils, some of them now teachers themselves. And when the World's Educational Convention met in London in 1854, she was present, as was her old friend Henry Barnard—both still committed to improving education.

Emma's brick house on the Troy Female Seminary's campus was well known to the hundreds of girls currently enrolled, as well as to hundreds of alumnae. She kept in touch with everything connected with the institution she had founded. In time she had five grandchildren. Nieces and nephews, great-nieces and great-nephews, as well as other young people, were always turning up, to Emma's great joy. She died in 1870 at the age of 87.

Twenty-one years later the Emma Willard Association was formed. It raised money for a huge bronze statue, the work of New York sculptor Alexander Doyle. It can be seen today in front of one of the Seminary buildings that was erected in 1895 and is now part of Russell Sage College. The Association's first scholarship was given to aid women at Middlebury College, coeducational since 1883, and the institution that inspired Emma to seek for women the type of higher education then open to men. This scholarship still exists. In 1905, Emma Willard was elected to the Hall of Fame for Great Americans, identifying her as one whose life had contributed significantly to human advancement.

To understand the importance of Emma Willard's role in American education, we must take a brief look at the nation's history.

In 1642 Massachusetts ruled that all children should be taught to read and write. A pamphlet printed the next year explains one crucial reason why the Puritans encouraged education:

AFTER GOD HAD CARRIED US SAFE TO NEW ENGLAND
AND WE HAD BUILDED OUR HOUSES
PROVIDED NECESSARIES FOR OUR LIVELIHOOD
REARED CONVENIENT PLACES FOR GOD'S WORSHIP
AND SETTLED THE CIVILL GOVERNMENT
ONE OF THE NEXT THINGS WE LONGED FOR
AND LOOKED AFTER WAS TO ADVANCE LEARNING
AND PERPETUATE IT TO PROSPERITY
DREADING TO LEAVE AN ILLITERATE MINISTRY
TO THE CHURCHES WHEN OUR PRESENT MINISTERS
SHALL LIE IN DUST.

With this in mind, they founded Harvard College in 1636.

By 1647 legislators were still worrying about the power of "that old deluder, Satan, to keep men from a knowledge of the Scriptures" and that learning might be "buried in the grave of our fathers in church and commonwealth." Thus they ordered that every town with 50 householders must provide a grammar school to fit youths for the university. This was the beginning of the move to public education, but it would take more than 200 years until all parts of the nation provided it. Most schools did not fit into what is now called either "public" or "independent" (private); for example, some were run by Moravians, Quakers, or other religious sects; some Southern home schools under a tutor; some were private schools for the rich; some were charity elementary schools for indigents, and so on. Apprenticeship training was sometimes given to orphans and children of the very poor. Also, legislative grants were often given to institutions of learning that were otherwise privately supported. (Emma referred to this practice in her Plan.) The concept of placing students in grades according to their progress was also slow in coming. In fact, what was probably the first real graded school in America did not come into being until 1847.

New England was a leader in education. Since Puritan theology laid great emphasis on reading and understanding the Bible, girls as well as boys were allowed to attend the so-called dame schools, where, for generations, young children 4 to 7 years of age learned to read and write. Usually these schools were in the homes of the teachers, and they cost very little. Sometimes the teacher was paid out of public funds. (In South Carolina, the wives of planters often taught girls in what was known as the Old Fields Schools.) The dame school along with the writing school, that taught writing and arithmetic, eventually became the elementary school. By 1807 most of New England states were offering free elementary education to girls. But the South was slow in converting to public education; it also had a high rate of illiteracy.

By the early 1800s the characteristic rural school was known as the district school—the type Emma attended in Connecticut. It was controlled locally, often under the guidance of clergymen, and financed by some combination of property taxes, fuel contributions, tuition payments and state aid. Children up to 14 and 16 attended some time during the year. Before mid-century, toddlers as young as three often accompanied their siblings. The number of pupils per teacher ranged from less than 40 to more than 100.

There were no individual desks—children were crowded on long, backless seats and benches. Blackboards were unknown until around 1809 and did not come into common use until 1820. (Slates were also available soon after that date.) Paper was expensive and therefore used sparingly.

Steel pens did not replace quills until around 1850, which meant that the teacher had to be skilled in making and repairing quill pens. Ink was of poor quality; a recipe used in Indiana, for instance, directed that it be made from maple bark, sumac, and oak balls, soaked in vinegar.

From an old catechism:

> What will be your condition in hell? *I shall be dreadfully tormented.* — What company will be there? *Legions of devils, and multitudes of sinners of the human race.*
>
> Will company afford me any comfort in hell? *It will not, but will probably increase my woes.*
>
> If you should go to hell, how long must you continue there? *For ever and ever.*
>
> If you should die in your sins, and God should make you miserable, should you have any reason to complain of him? *Not the least. I must be speechless.*

From *Old-Time Schools and School-Books* by Clifton Johnson, 1904.

Generally speaking, textbooks were in short supply. Sometimes the children studied from texts belonging to their families. In the latter situation, there was no uniformity in the books used, and most were generations old. Often primers were available only to the teachers. This necessitated that a group gather round the instructor as he pointed out with a quill the words he desired a given child to read aloud. The scarcity of books encouraged rote memorization.

The subjects taught were reading, writing, arithmetic, grammar and geography. Bible reading and catechism recitation were part of the learning process. Moral education was stressed at every turn, with the Protestant ethic dominant. Textbooks glorified the Republic and all it did. Children learned respect for their elders and to "make their manners" by bowing and curtsying.

Since corporal punishment was the rule of the day, it was believed that male rather than female teachers should keep order and control obstinate students. Thus it was usual for men teachers to cover winter sessions, held from December to March. At this time well-educated farmers in the community were sometimes free to teach. However, during the summer sessions, between April and September, when children over the age of ten were usually doing farm work, women were employed to instruct the very young children. Emma, it will be recalled, was one of these.

Between 1800 and 1830 the Lancasterian system was popular in many common schools; an older student was used to train groups of younger children. The system facilitated the teaching of a large number of pupils under one teacher. However, it depended largely on rote.

The district schools were primitive constructions, supposed to be centrally located, and usually built on land of little value—with no shade trees to provide protection from wind and sun. Here are Emma's own words about the school she attended:

> The school was a place of rude structure; but be it remembered, it was fully as good as the dwelling houses. The children were not enervated by luxuries at home. They came on a cold winter morning, trooping along, with the ruddy glow of health and exercise. The boys had fed the cattle, the girls had milked the cows, and made the beds in rooms which no fireplace or stove had ever disturbed; and now the bounding pulse of life beat high and strong in their veins; and they minded little the unwarmed condition of the meeting house on Sunday, or the whistling of the wind through the crevices of the school house on week days. . . . If no backs were provided for their seats in school, neither were there any at home to the blocks in ample chimney corners upon which those favored few were privileged to sit.

The grammar schools were instituted to prepare boys for college. Although this nation's colleges came into being to provide education chiefly for the clergy, it was also recognized that lawyers, teachers and government servants should receive higher education too. Despite the fact that Noah Webster of dictionary fame advocated less adherence to the European-type education that extolled the classics, these colleges still put great emphasis on Latin and Greek. They were located mainly in cities and did not admit girls. The teachers were, of course, men, most of whom had a college education. These grammar schools flourished in New England; other states desired a more practical type of education for boys. (We should note that the curriculum of nineteenth-century colleges and secondary schools differed markedly from modern programs, chiefly because of changes in the body of knowledge.) Eventually most of the Latin grammar schools were supplanted by academies and high schools. But in the nineteenth century only a minority of teenagers received any type of education. With a few exceptions, slave children received no education at all.

When Emma finished at her district school, the only type of higher education open to her was in private schools. The Moravian Academies in Bethlehem, Pennsylvania, and Winston Salem, North Carolina, the Union School in New Haven, Connecticut, and Miss Pierce's Academy in Litchfield, Connecticut, were among some of the better schools. These secondary schools almost always charged fees, and very often girls had to live away from home to attend them. But circumstances of course made it difficult for poor girls to obtain something approaching a high school education. There were also many private "female seminaries" of lower quality. Such schools were prone to emphasize showy accomplishments — painting, elocution, musical perfection and the like — to the neglect of the academic subjects taught to males. This was the type of school Emma deplored. Economically they were ofteen shaky, sometimes exploitive and usually unable to survive for many more than a few years.

Most people deemed the type of education offered by the female seminaries adequate. According to Noah Webster, "That education is always wrong which raises woman above the duties of her station. . . ." To justify such thinking we should remember that in the developing Republic, manpower was needed for all sorts of pursuits, and it was expected that a woman marry and bear a large number of children. Maintaining a home and raising a family required so much time and energy, there was little concern about her education. And with the Bible the bedrock of life, everyone believed that what God said to Eve applied to all women: ". . . and thy desire shall be to thy husband, And he shall rule over thee." Horace Mann, the distinguished educator from Massachusetts, wrote in 1845: "Four-fifths of all the women who have ever lived, have been the slaves of men, — menials in his household, the drudges in his field, the instruments of his pleasure; or, at best, the gilded toys of his leisure days in court or palace." In such an atmosphere, a system that underscored the social graces was acceptable; if women were to be educated, they did not need subjects that would admit them to college.

Nevertheless, there had been suggestions that this state of affairs left something to be desired. Benjamin Rush, physician and signer of the Declaration of Independence, had urged serious education of girls, while the spirited Abigail Adams, wife of the second president and mother of the sixth, advocated equal educational opportunities for women. And there were others — but only a handful — who held such views. It was 1824 before the first girls' public high school opened in Worcester, Massachusetts. Throughout the first 75 years of the nineteenth century, the seminary predominated the education of women. Thomas Woody, an authority on women's education, contends that "in the female seminary, women had their first general opportunity to gain intellectual insight into the problems of life. No longer were they compelled to rely wholly on the hard experience gained from everyday drudgery. It is on the foundation of seminary education that women built a superstructure of a higher education and prepared for manifold activities in various professions."

He notes that the success of the old private seminary contributed to the development of the public high school and the female college. Emma was, of course, a prime mover in the development of good female seminaries. An illustration of Troy's excellence is provided by a statement from the six male scholars chosen as the Examination Committee for 1845.

They observed that Emma's school had "the same superiority over the other Female Seminaries which Harvard and Yale have over colleges of more recent date."

Emma also showed foresight in recognizing the growing need for the teachers in common schools. The nation's first compulsory school law was enacted by Massachusetts in 1852 and began enforced school attendance. Between 1830 and 1860 five million foreigners were added to the United States population. Finally it was clear to all that trained teachers were desperately needed.

The life of a woman teacher left much to be desired. In rural areas teachers of both sexes were expected to "board round" in the families of their pupils, and the value of this was subtracted from their wages. Women were almost always paid less than men. An illustration from Michigan is fairly typical: in 1845 in that state, women teachers' salaries averaged 44 percent of males'. And women were still usually relegated to teaching young children in the common schools. But is was a beginning. According to Woody, ". . . having secured admission to the lowliest of public professions — that of teaching — women gradually forced their way into the most exclusive professional fields of medicine, law, and even sacred theology."

Emma's concept of a woman's sphere as distinct from that of a man is in direct conflict with the modern feminist viewpoint; indeed it did not please the feminists of her own day. She was deeply religious and apparently took the Bible literally:

> I would not be understood to insinuate that we are not, in particular situations, to yield obedience to the other sex. Submission and obedience belong to every being in the universe, except the great master of the whole. Nor is it a degrading peculiarity to our sex to be under human authority. Whenever one class of human beings derive from another the benefit of support and protection, they must pay its equivalent — obedience.

And again: "St. Paul has said they [women] must not speak in churches, but he has nowhere said they must not speak in school houses. To men is given the duty of providing for children, to women that of applying to their use this provision. . . ."

In her Plan she almost apologized for wanting to educate women: "The absurdity of sending ladies to college may, at first thought, strike everyone to whom this subject shall be proposed. I therefore hasten to observe that the seminary here recommended will be as different from those appropriated to the other sex as the female character and duties are from the male." She advocated the education of women not for their own sakes, as much as for the benefit of the young Republic she loved so dearly; educated mothers would train their sons better than would ignorant mothers. And she seems to have believed that women teachers should be trained primarily because their country needed them, and secondarily because they needed careers. (She assumed, but may not have approved, that they would accept lower salaries than their male counterparts.) For many years she drew attention to the fact that the talents of women were needed if the Republic were to prosper. Of course in that era many citizens were proud of the fledgling nation and worried about its survival; but such sentiments will seem odd to an egocentric generation.

The advancement of female education was so important to Emma that she refused to ally herself with what was then considered the radical suffrage movement. (Ironically, one of its leaders, Elizabeth Cady Stanton, was a graduate of Troy Female Seminary, class of 1832.)

It is clear that Emma believed in an *educated white* electorate. She regarded blacks as inferior to whites; in fact, she considered their color as a sign from God that they were inferior. But she disapproved of separating black families. She favored sending Negroes to Liberia; otherwise, she would keep them here in a condition of "regulated servitude, not slavery, for man belongs to God, not a human master." To someone so patriotic, saving the union at almost any cost was imperative. Henry Clay, because of his efforts to compromise in order to keep the nation together, was a personal hero. After the secession of South Carolina, she gathered signatures from 4000 women for a memorial petitioning Congress for peace. Secretary of State William Seward criticized it as advocating slavery.

Her patriotism extended to a fear that the European immigrants would undermine the country's institutions, and that Mormons posed a danger by

> allowing that people to organize a State with their peculiar institutions; and I feel the more of this subject as the progress of the sect involves, as I have reason to believe, the degradation of my own sex, and, if of my sex, certainly the deterioration of the whole of society. We were born a Protestant Christian nation . . . If we tolerate others that is enough. We should not allow them to form governments or exercise political powers on any other basis. If they want to do this, let them go elsewhere . . .

Though Emma did not work actively for female suffrage, she had a clear understanding of the importance of women in the national welfare. To a friend she wrote, "The state can no more do without woman's tenderness and motherly wisdom than can the family. That I have been preaching all my life . . . ." And even before the first woman's convention in Seneca Falls, New York, in 1848, she had written:

> As a human being walks in safety with both his limbs, while with one only he hobbles and is in constant danger of falling; so has human government, forgetting that God has made two sexes, depended for its movements hitherto on one alone. The march of human improvement is scarce a proper term to express its past progress, since in order to march, both limbs are required.

Despite Emma's insistence on the proper sphere for a woman, does not the following seem peculiarly modern? It was written to a niece in 1844.

> I hope you will not drop your pen, and shut up your piano, and make your education to no avail, because you have a child. A little resolution is needed to find or make time, and that is all that is necessary. Mrs. John Willard, with five children, performs well the duties of principal of the school.

In 1857 Emma's *Morals for the Young* stated: "In making her calculations for the future, . . . every woman is wise to prepare herself to become independent, useful and happy, without marriage; although her education should always fit her for those high and holy duties, which result from marriage and maternity." Here she returns to the thesis that women should be educated to become good wives and mothers. And she liked to point out that the life of a teacher is far better than that of a factory operative.

She was backed up in these ideas by Catherine Beecher (1800–1887). Miss Beecher devoted most of her adult life to educating women for all phases of family life; she also worked indefatigably for the training of competent teachers. Her contribution to the education of women ranks in importance with that of Emma and Mary Lyon, whom we shall meet shortly.

Emma Willard will not be remembered for some of her political and social advocacies. But she made significant progress in obtaining equality in education for women. By the time she died, Mount Holyoke, Elmira, Mary Sharp, Wesleyan Female and other colleges for women were in existence, while such institutions as Oberlin, Antioch, Iowa State and the University of Utah provided co-education. In fact, John Lord in 1873 was able to note in the introduction to Emma's biography, "At last woman is educated as well or better than her husband or brother; this is an immense stride in civilization."

This advance in education should not be overlooked. In 1929 Woody wrote: "Looking back over the past hundred years, it is clear . . . that though political emancipation is the great symbol of women's victory, their intellectual emancipation, because of its priority and fundamental character, was of vaster significance." Perhaps this exonerates Emma's failure to work for women's suffrage.

Mary Lyon
Mount Holyoke College

Mount Holyoke College in South Hadley, Massachusetts, today ranks as one of the foremost educational institutions in the United States. Its founder was Mary Lyon, and this chapter tells her story.

Mary Mason Lyon was born on February 28, 1797, in the town of Buckland, located in western Massachusetts. She was the sixth of eight children of Aaron and Jemima (Shepard) Lyon, and was descended from farmers and craftsmen men as well as ministers and deacons. At the time of her birth, both parents were Baptists and religion was a major part of their lives.

Her father died when Mary was almost six. For the next seven years, Jemima, with the help of her children, managed to run the family farm. Then in 1810, she married a widower in need of a wife to care for his five young children. When she moved to her new home in nearby Ashfield, she took with her only her youngest children. Her son Aaron, then 21, stayed on at the Lyon farm with Mary to keep house for him until he married. Housekeeping was no small feat, especially for a 13-year old; there was churning to be done, soap and candles to be made, wool to be spun and woven into clothing—and so on. For her efforts her brother paid her one silver dollar a week, and this she saved. Mary remained devoted to Jemima until the latter's death. She wrote many letters to her mother, often requesting her prayers on various matters. However, she apparently did not regard her stepfather's home as a place she might visit as a daughter.

Mary probably went to district schools in Buckland and Ashland, but details about her early education are lacking. She was still a Baptist at this time (she joined the Congregational Church later). Through the church she heard about Americans who were going overseas as missionaries. This was the beginning of her interest in the foreign mission field, and even in her youth there were signs of the burning religious zeal that would guide her life and play an important role in the history of Mount Holyoke College.

In 1814, at the recommendation of one of her teachers, the 17-year-old Mary was hired to teach the 20-week summer session in the school at Shelburne Falls. Of course "boarding round" was part of the bargain, and she found herself living for four weeks at the home of each of her five pupils.

Mary Lyon. Painting by Joseph Goodhue Chandler. Courtesy Mount Holyoke College Art Museum.

In addition to this type of board, her weekly recompense was 75 cents. The following summer she taught at the same school, and it is likely that for the next ten years she taught other summer sessions in the Buckland area.

When Sanderson Academy opened in Ashfield in the fall of 1817, Mary used most of her resources, including articles she had spun or woven, to pay for a term's tuition and a place to board. At the school she became friendly with Amanda White, the oldest daughter of Thomas White, who was a trustee of the Academy and one of Ashfield's prominent citizens. She had no money for a second term, but her academic ability had impressed Mr. White so much that he seems to have persuaded his fellow trustees to grant her free tuition. In addition, he and his wife opened their home to her so that she did not have to worry about money for board. Mary's friendship with the members of the White family was to be a lasting one; Mr. White became financial advisor to her, Amanda and she attended Byfield Seminary together, and a younger sister named Hannah later taught under Mary's supervision.

The year 1818 saw Mary attending the coeducational Amherst Academy for a term. She studied rhetoric, logic and chemistry. To pay her way she drew on part of the small sum of money due her from her father's estate. Her biographers imply that she had less interest in her appearance than in opportunities to develop her mind. They describe her as a large-framed, robust woman with blue eyes and red hair. She appears to have had great energy, was considered good natured and known to possess a sense of humor. She stated herself that memorization was easy for her. Nevertheless, her continued struggle to gain knowledge distinguished her among her female contemporaries.

After holding a variety of teaching jobs, Mary still yearned to learn more. An opportunity came in 1821 when Amanda White was planning to enter a new seminary for young ladies, run by the Rev. Joseph Emerson. It was located in Byfield, Massachusetts, in the northeastern part of the state—a three-day journey from Buckland. Mary decided to invest everything she had in several months' study at Byfield Academy, and went there with Amanda.

It was a wise decision. She was then 24 and found herself among some students as old and mature as herself; some had taught also, and some were hoping to teach or become missionaries. She soon formed a friendship with one of the teachers, Zilpah Polly Grant from Connecticut. Mary's new friend was gracious and charming and well liked, as well as deeply religious. She would have a significant effect on Mary's professional career.

Some of the material covered at Byfield was not new to Mary, but Emerson's enthusiasm and philosophy intrigued her. He was a religious man who based his trust on the Bible, and his profound conviction made a lasting impression on Mary. Naturally a believer such as he encouraged the propagation of the faith through missions, and his approval spurred Mary's initial interest. But Emerson was not a tolerant Christian; he worked for religious conversion among his students, and, like many of his generation, saw little to commend in Catholicism and the liberal Unitarianism. His puritanical prejudice extended to novels of the day and to much conventional literature. On the other hand, in 1822, when women's education was not a burning issue, he expressed hope that the time would come when female institutions would exist and "be considered as important, as are now our colleges for the education of our sons."

According to Amanda her friend was "gaining knowledge by the hand-fuls" at Byfield. Emerson himself noted later that in sheer mental power, Mary was the best student who had ever attended his school.

Thomas White saw to it that when Mary had finished at Byfield she became second-in-command at Sanderson Academy, where she had once been both student and part-time teacher. This was a feat, because never before had a woman been hired for a position of responsibility. Here Mary remained for two years, teaching under Dartmouth graduates on their way to better things.

One of Mary's friends at Amherst Academy had married a Congregational minister named Edward Hitchcock. Hitchcock was a scholar and former teacher. The Hitchcocks were living in Conway, a town close to both Ashfield and Amherst, and in the summer of 1823 Mary lived in their home. Besides teaching in a private school, she studied science with Edward and also painting and drawing with his wife Orra. Edward Hitchcock would become a professor and later president at the recently established Amherst College and in time, a founder of the American Association for the Advancement of Science. He would have a longtime association with Mary Lyon and Mount Holyoke College.

And now a new opening presented itself to the young and ambitious Mary. Zilpah Grant from Byfield Academy had been appointed principal of a new school in Londonderry, just north of the Massachusetts border. In 1824 Mary joined her as an assistant at Adams Female Academy, drawing a salary of $5 a week plus board, for a summer term of 30 weeks. The school had three levels of classes and the girls were placed in them according to the knowledge they displayed, rather than by their previous school attendance.

The following year Mary had an opportunity to improve her science teaching. At Amherst College she had heard lectures by Amos Eaton, the same professor who had taught Emma Willard. When she wrote him concerning the instruction of chemistry, he suggested that she come to Troy to visit his Rensselaer Institute, and this she did. This is another example of Mary's determination to acquire knowledge, despite a heavy teaching schedule and very little money.

Since the Adams school was not open in winter, Mary continued her practice of winter teaching in and around Buckland; she was in reality a year-round teacher in an era when teaching was exceptionally demanding. Increasing registration in her schools attested to her success. By 1825 she had a private school with an enrollment close to 50, and hired one of the White girls, Hannah, to help her. A letter written at this time shows that girls attending a "select" school away from home might have problems about where to live. These are Mary's words:

Fourteen of my scholars board in the family with me. Before I came here, and for the first week after, I had much anxiety about the arrangements for these young ladies. We have finally become settled, so that everything seems to go well. The members of the school in the family have a table by themselves. As I was well aware that it would require much more than an ordinary share of dignity to prevent too much, if not improper, conversation at meals, I thought it the safest to introduce some entertaining exercise.

In 1830 the winter school had about 100 girls. They came not only from Massachusetts, but also Connecticut and Vermont. Mary was now training them to teach in the common schools, and it was not unusual for school committee members to look to her classes for prospective teachers.

Zilpah Grant saw to it that religious instruction occupied one-seventh of her school's curriculum. Mary wholeheartedly approved of this, encouraging the conversion of all her pupils at both Londonderry and Buckland. When a religious revival swept one of her winter schools, she feared that the girls might become "so absorbed in their studies, so much interested in the business of the school, as to exclude God from their hearts. . . ." Later she wrote of 11 girls who were "professedly pious" and that "I have had a faint hope, through the winter, that this town, and my school might be visited by the special influence of the Holy Spirit." When Adams Academy experienced a revival in 1826, Mary stated that of the 90 pupils: "Only a small proportion profess religion or hope that they are Christians. Nearly eighty are living without God in the world. At this period, when so many spiritual blessings are bestowed in literary institutions, may we not hope that ours may be among the favored number? Many Christians, parents and others, have been interested for this institution. We hope their prayers will be answered. . . ." Although conversions were a source of joy to Mary and Zilpah, some of the trustees at Adams Academy were not so impressed. In New England the Calvinism supported by these women was under attack by the more moderate Unitarianism. The executive committee of the board declared:

> It was the original design of the trustees to establish this seminary on liberal principles. They regret that the institution has acquired the character of being strictly Calvinistic in the religious instruction. This character has grown up in opposition to the sentiments and wishes of a majority of the trustees. It is their determination to select persons who will not attempt to instil into the minds of their pupils the peculiar tenets of any denomination of Christians, but will give the general instruction wherein all Christians agree.

Another source of contention was the teaching of dancing, supported by the board but against Zilpah's principles. By January 1828 she had dissolved her connection with Adams Female Academy. But very soon she headed a new school in Ipswich, Massachusetts, 25 miles from Boston. The departure of its principal with many of the students caused Adams to close, but Ipswich continued to prosper until 1839. By 1830, Mary had agreed to year-round work there as assistant principal, remaining until the fall of 1834.

The waxing and waning of female academies, as illustrated by Mary's experience, are an indication of the problems involving secondary education for women during the first half of the nineteenth century. Emma Willard, as we have seen, recognized very early in her career the need for endowed institutions, and Catherine Beecher, whom we have mentioned previously as one of the era's leading lights in female education, worked unflaggingly to obtain continuing financial support. Mary Lyon also would soon be working for permanent funding of a women's educational institute of collegiate grade.

In 1831 there were almost 200 students enrolled at Ipswich Female Seminary/Academy, 20 of them transfers from Mary's school in Buckland. Ipswich offered no so-called ornamental branches. Although classics were not taught, there was concentration on other solid subjects. To illustrate, by 1834 the science classes included chemistry, physics, astronomy, botany, biology, geology and physiology. But as early as 1831 vocal music, not commonly in a school's curriculum, was being taught under the direction of Lowell Mason, familiar today as the composer of "Nearer My God to Thee" and other hymns. The students boarded with families in town, and it was clear that the large enrollment was difficult to accommodate. After 1831 the school declined to accept girls less than 11 years old, and eventually it was in a position to impose entrance requirements. Calisthenics was a requisite and, of course, Bible study. The practice of bringing souls to Christ continued unabated. An article in the *American Annals of Education* complimented the system devised by Zilpah and Mary, and their graduates were in demand as teachers in several states.

Mary was now an experienced teacher with definite ideas about education. Her correspondence shows her familiarity with many textbooks of the day and gives her reasons for approving or rejecting them. One of her students at this time and who later became a colleague and confidante, gave this important insight, which she wrote after Mary's death:

> She aimed to teach her pupils to educate themselves, to show them how to study, to help them lay the foundation of an edifice which they were themselves to finish.... To go *through* a book, she considered a matter of little consequence. To see it well begun, to set her pupils' minds on the right track, to open them fields of investigation, was in her view the main business.

In addition to being considered a first-class teacher, she was "regarded by all as a general friend and advisor."

As assistant principal Mary had numerous administrative duties. These became onerous as Zilpah was absent for long periods because of real or supposed ill health. One of her troubles was an ankle injury that kept her on crutches for several years. Her illnesses — psychosomatic or physical — forced more and more managerial responsibility on Mary; in fact, she was acting head for almost two years. This undoubtedly made her confident that she could run her own school.

Zilpah and Mary both wished for a permanent endowment for Byfield, even if it meant moving the school elsewhere. In 1831 they suggested in writing to the trustees that ladies be afforded the same situation as young men in attending colleges and other seminaries; they wanted a rent-free instructional building with suitable facilities, as well as a boarding house to accommodate 150. At first their proposal stimulated some interest, but it was short lived. Also, Zilpah was away again recuperating, and consequently of little help to the project. A year later, at the suggestion of trustee George Heard, Mary drew up an outline for what she called the New England Seminary for Teachers. This institution was to be strictly evangelical and of high scholastic standard. The plan saw print but apparently had little impact. By 1833 Mary was writing Zilpah that if the proposal were to become reality, "Many good men will fear the effect on society of so much female influence, and what they call female greatness."

Late in 1832 Mary learned that a boys' school in Amherst, located on 15 acres of land, was for sale or rent. For three months she tried hard to stimulate interest in moving the Ipswich operation to Amherst, but it was a losing battle. She was, however, now determined to have a permanently endowed school, even if it meant leaving Ipswich and raising funds on her own. She wrote to Zilpah as follows:

> If I should separate from you, I have no definite plan. But my thoughts, feelings, and judgment are turned toward the middle class of society. For this class I want to labor, and for this class I consider myself peculiarly fitted to labor. To this class in society would I devote, directly, all the remainder of my strength (God permitting) — not to the higher classes, not to the poorer classes. This middle class contains the main springs, and main wheels, which are to move the world. . . .
>
> I view it (Ipswich) just like Mr. Emerson's school. It was very important that Mr. Emerson should prosper during his days of labor, and that he should have a place where he put forth his strength to peculiar advantage. But where is his school now?

This last sentence expresses her concern over the fact that institutions too often flourished under personalities, but perished when these dominating influences were gone. So her aim was to establish an enduring seminary, and with this in view she made arrangements to leave Ipswich by September 1834. To her mother she wrote:

> I have been for a great while thinking about those young ladies who find it necessary to make such an effort for their education as I made, when I obtained mine. In one respect, from year to year, I have not felt quite satisfied with my present field of labor. I have desired to be in a school, the expenses of which would be so small, that many who are now discouraged from endeavoring to enjoy the privileges of this, might be favored with those which are similar at less expense. The course of instruction adopted in this institution, and the course which I have endeavored to adopt when I have instructed among my native hills, I believe is eminently suited to make good mothers as well as teachers.

To a sister she wrote:

> I am about to embark in a frail boat on a boisterous sea. I know not whither I shall be driven, nor how I shall be tossed, nor to what port I shall aim . . . But I am not anxious . . . I never had a prospect of engaging in any labor which seemed so directly the work of the Lord as this. It is very sweet, in the midst of the darkness and doubt, to commit the whole to his guidance.

During the summer of 1833 Mary traveled for three-and-a-half months, venturing as far west as Detroit. Using various means of transportation, she covered more than 2000 miles. Besides visiting relatives and friends, she went sightseeing, observed many schools and institutions and called on educators. The latter included Emma Willard, but nothing is recorded about the meeting. In Philadelphia she met Angelina Grimké, who was to become prominent in both the abolitionist and woman's movements.

Zilpah certainly knew and apparently approved of Mary's plan to found an institution not unlike Ipswich, but whose fees would be much less, and the biography by Elizabeth Alden Green points out that the campaign for Mount Holyoke College was launched from Zilpah's seminary. This took place in February 1834 with the issue of a printed appeal for funds and was addressed "To Friends and Patrons of Ipswich Female Seminary." Seven months later some ministers and other men of influence, meeting at Ipswich, formed a committee to establish the school that Mary envisioned. The year before, she had written to Zilpah, "I feel more and more that the whole business must, in name, devolve on benevolent gentlemen. . . ." Now she was making sure the public perceived that the responsibility for the school lay in male, not female hands. But during her last few weeks with Zilpah, Mary herself solicited about $1000 from teachers, students and townswomen.

Mr. Heard was a member of that original committee, as was the Rev. Theophilus Packard, an Amherst college trustee who had previously served in the same capacity at Williams College. The Rev. Roswell Hanks was also recruited, and these three men were excellent fundraisers. Professor Hitchcock of Amherst was a member too. The latter would serve as a trustee of Mount Holyoke from 1836 to 1864, and over the years gave Mary much valued advice. Through him and others Mount Holyoke had close ties to Amherst. Mary resided with the Hitchcock family much of the time between her departure from the Ipswich school and the building of Mount Holyoke. There is also evidence that she taught Latin to some of their children while she lived there.

Early in 1835 South Hadley had been chosen as the site. A year later Mount Holyoke Female Seminary was incorporated by the state of Massachusetts. Within a few months, the cornerstone of the building had been laid. The grounds consisted of about 15 acres, located in a scenic area near the Connecticut River and Mount Holyoke. Andrew Porter, a cotton mill owner in Monson and a trustee, helped immeasurably in (superintending) the construction of the building. Daniel Safford of Boston, a prosperous ironworks owner, was enlisted by Mary to raise money. He was most successful in this undertaking. He remained on the board and made large personal contributions until his death in 1856. The wives of both these men liked and admired Mary, and she was a frequent guest in their homes.

The trustees would change, and there would be constant necessity to raise money, but dedicated men always came forward to meet the challenge. There is no doubt that they had faith in Mary Lyon, and it is also clear that directly or indirectly, she was the prime mover of the Mount Holyoke project, which had become almost an obsession with her.

After leaving Ipswich Seminary she devoted a large portion of her time to fundraising. This involved both writing and traveling as she sought and interviewed prospective donors. Late in 1836 she involved herself in the acquisition of furnishings for the dormitory rooms. Her plan was to have a dependable woman in a given area collect either cash or materials sufficient for one room. Mary soon found that she did better if she appeared in person to plead her cause. Here is a letter written in 1837 by a young woman living in Heath, Massachusetts:

> We have been favored with a visit from Miss Lyon, she interested us much in behalf of her Sem. I believe with you that no one can hear her speak upon the subject without having their feelings enlisted in favor of the cause. Will you believe me when I tell you the people in Heath gave $1200 for the Sem. She presented the subject in such a manner that no one could fail grasping it at once, she removed all objections so that many

who decided not to give before seeing her, cheerfully subscribed $50 . . . the ladies here will probably furnish a room.

Essential as fundraising was, Mary had to think about recruiting students and faculty. There was also the curriculum to plan as well as the organization of the domestic life of the institution. Besides all this, she had decisions to make about the actual construction of the edifice going up according to her specifications. Fortunately a couple who lived close to the building invited her to stay with them during the last three months of construction.

During this period Mary also had a major part in the establishment of Wheaton Seminary. In 1834 Judge Laban Wheaton of Norton, Massachusetts, lost his only daughter. He was persuaded by his daughter-in-law to found as a memorial a first-rate school for girls. The Wheatons knew of Mary and sought her advice. As a temporary principal she recommended Eunice Caldwell who had graduated from Ipswich Seminary and afterwards had taught there and in Philadelphia. Eunice was also a personal friend of Zilpah and Mary's, and Mary was lining her up to be the first assistant principal at Mount Holyoke.

After Wheaton Seminary (now College) opened in 1835, Mary often stayed there. Student letters in 1836–37 indicate that Mary was a visiting teacher at that institution. She and their principal must have impressed the girls, for between 1836–37 Wheaton teachers and students, then numbering around 50, contributed $235 towards furnishing a parlor at Mary Lyon's school.

November 8, 1837, was chosen for the opening, despite the fact that the country was suffering from a severe financial depression that year. The four-story brick building that cost $15,000 still lacked steps to the doors; some furniture and bedding had not arrived; and there were other inconveniences. But none of this deterred Mary or the trustees and their wives who were helping out with various menial tasks. Mary stuck to her original plan for providing low board and tuition, setting it at $64 for a 40-week session. Some expense was defrayed by the requirement that each girl take part in the domestic work of what Mary called her family. In short, there were no servants, since cooking, cleaning and laundry as well as hauling and fetching were done by the 80 girls who arrived that year. Mary put great emphasis on physical exercise for the students and considered the domestic work part of this. She felt that it imparted a spirit of democracy. All students were required to live in. Although South Hadley residents had contributed $8000, Mary was adamant that no girl should receive special consideration such as being allowed to attend as a day student. Mary herself would not accept more than $200 plus board and heat, and this set a standard for her subordinates. (In contrast, Catherine Beecher had offered Zilpah $1000 a year to become co-head at Catherine's Hartford Female Seminary.)

During the 1830s there appeared in print expressions of Mary's principles and her design for Mount Holyoke College. Here are some excerpts of her own writing.

> [Mount Holyoke] is to be principally devoted to the preparing of female teachers. At the same time, it will qualify ladies for other spheres of usefulness. The design is to give a solid, extensive, and well-balanced English education.

> This institution is to be founded on the high principle of enlarged Christian benevolence. In its plan and its appeals it seeks no support from local or private interest. It is designed entirely for the public good, and the trustees would adopt no measures not in accordance with this design. It is sacredly consecrated to the great Head of the church, and they would not seek for human approbation by any means which will not be well pleasing in his sight. The institution is designed to be permanent.

> The institution is to be entirely for an older class of young ladies. The general system for family arrangements, for social improvement, for the division of time, for the organizing and regulating the school, and the requirements for entrance, will be adapted throughout to young ladies of adult age and mature character.

> The friends of this seminary have sought that this might be a spot where souls be born of God, and where much shall be done for maturing and elevating the Christian character.

> But it is not enough that a great number of ladies are well educated. They must also have benevolence enough to engage in teaching, when other duties will allow and when their labors are needed. Female teachers should not expect to be fully compensated for their services, unless it be by kindness and gratitude.

> The spirit of this seminary is suited not only to increase the number of educated ladies, but to enforce on them the obligation to use their talents for the good of others, especially in teaching. It is hoped it may also lead them to be more willing to take any school and in any place where their services are most needed.

At first, Mount Holyoke's academic standard resembled that of Ipswich Seminary's three-year course. Mary held firmly that her entering students must have emotional maturity; she refused to admit anyone under 16 and preferred older students. There were also entrance examinations to be passed, as well as public examinations at each year's end. Willystine Goodsell, an authority on education notes that: "The student of educational history will perhaps recognize the close similarity between the initial curriculum of Mount Holyoke and that of the English and scientific courses offered in certain colleges for men of the same period." (The classics were not offered and the level of mathematics was below that of the men's colleges.) As noted earlier, it is difficult to compare the standard to that of a modern college.

Mary continually improved the standard of her school. She very soon began to plan for a fourth year, although this did not materialize until 1862. By 1893 the institution was officially designated a college. Latin, which was still considered by some the most important subject of advanced education, was required for graduation as early as 1846.

Mount Holyoke was a success from the beginning. There were always more applications than spaces, so an addition to the building was started in 1840. By 1847 the enrollment was 235, with more than that number turned away for lack of accommodation. Another wing was built after Mary's death in 1849, and additional buildings began to appear. Today Mount Holyoke College, which remains independent, provides an excellent education in the liberal arts for more than 1800 students, and has a campus of 800 acres. Mary Lyon's dream has been fulfilled, and her college is the oldest continuing institution of higher education for women in the United States.

Dormitory life in Mary's day was very different from that enjoyed by today's college student. It was not until mid-century that waterclosets and hot and cold running water were installed on each floor, and their lack necessitated trips to outhouses and the carrying of slops and water in pails. Wood-burning stoves in the rooms required carrying also (each student paid for her wood), and fire was an ever-present danger. There were rules governing almost everything, and from 5 a.m. until 10 p.m., the student's life was run by bells that signified specific assignments. Mary did not approve of novel reading; she also had a prejudice against the use of both tea and coffee. Promptness was required, while speaking above a whisper was discouraged in the halls and other parts of the building. Infringements of rules were supposed to be self-reported, and there was also much policing. Staying out all night, of course, was likely to cause immediate expulsion. Nevertheless, most students seemed to enjoy Mount Holyoke and to revere its head. And there seems to have been little dissatisfaction with food; during the first term one girl wrote: "Dinner is made up of roasted beef, codfish, and the like, and always a second course of dumplings, pies or puddings. Supper of bread and butter, sauce, and cake or gingerbread. So you see we live well, yet all is plain."

Should the reader be entertaining the idea that Mary Lyon was repressive, here are some samples of Harvard Faculty votes in 1846–47.

Voted: That Plympton, Junior, be privately admonished for whistling in the South Entry Of U. Hall, on Wednesday A.M., May 13th.

> **Voted:** That Webb, Senior, be privately admonished for tardiness at chapel Service, Sunday A.M., May 17.
>
> **Voted:** That Bonaparte, Junior, be publicly admonished for having the game of cock-fighting at his room on Fast Day, and that Johnson I, Junior, be told that he also would be publicly admonished for being present at said game, if he were not on probation.
>
> **Voted:** That Porter, Junior, be dismissed from the college unless he shall, within a reasonable time, satisfy the President that he was not guilty of gross immorality in having two females in his room at midnight of the 20th instant.

Despite rules and regulations, the students in some male colleges had reputations for disorderliness and rebellion; drunken riots were not unknown.

In 1840 about 40 Mount Holyoke students contracted typhoid fever; nine of them died. It is likely that typhoid bacilli from a carrier contaminated either water or unpasteurized milk. But at that time, the bacterial nature of the disease was not recognized, so effective prevention could not be practiced. It is clear that the girls became infected before they left school for the holidays, though they became sick at their homes. Some students were afraid to enroll for the next semester, but their places were promptly filled by people on the long waiting list. So the new seminary survived a serious threat to its existence, and continued to prosper under Mary's leadership.

Student deaths on the school premises were not unknown. With the communication and transportation of the day, sometimes a parent (usually the father) did not arrive in time. Mary made a practice of caring for dying students herself, staying with then and comforting them until the end.

In 1849 she nursed a young woman who was dying of erysipelas, which is caused by a streptococcus. At the time Mary was 52 and still playing a very active role in the administration of Mount Holyoke; but her health seems to have been on the decline. At any rate, she died of erysipelas. Fifty-six years later, she was honored by election to the Hall of Fame for Great Americans.

Today Mary Lyon is recognized as an innovative and farsighted educator. Little is said about the religion that ruled her life and had impact on the early history of the seminary she founded. It should be recognized that religion played a major part in the life of the nineteenth century, and many parents were very pleased to send their daughters to an institution dedicated to saving souls. Mary held the Calvinistic view that an individual is depraved until he acknowledges Christ as his personal savior. With such a belief she naturally promoted revivals, prayed for conversions and extolled missionary activities. But despite her personal convictions, Mount Holyoke remained non-sectarian, and non-believers seem not to have been unduly harassed. On admission, a student declared herself as a professing Christian, or indulging hope or without hope.

Every year, Mary contributed $90 out of her salary of $200 to the American Board of Commissioners of Foreign Missionaries. She also encouraged her teachers and pupils to do likewise, and during the 1840s Mount Holyoke's annual gift to foreign and home missionaries averaged $1000. Her influence in this respect was clearly stated by a student in 1844:

> Yesterday a subscription was passed in behalf of the missionary cause. Miss Lyon is the most interested person in this cause I ever saw. It seems to be her chief desire and prayer that she may cultivate to a high degree the same spirit in all under her care. Her efforts have been greatly successful. Her scholars are scattered all over the world as missionaries and in other fields of usefulness. Her heart and hand are ever open to do good.

The Missionary Board preferred to recruit married rather than single women for service abroad. However, when it chose Fidelia Fiske, one of Mount Holyoke's most able teachers, who happened to be single, Mary drove through 30 miles of snowdrifts to persuade Miss Fiske's mother that her daughter was needed in Persia (now Iran). There were even a few instances when Mount Holyoke girls married, after extremely brief acquaintanceships, young ministers bound for foreign lands but lacking mates. Some of these young women met tragic ends. In 1839 one of them, only 20, sailed with her husband to Smyrna (now Izmir, Turkey) and was dead three months later. Another member of the first class left for West Africa in 1841. She, too, was dead within three months. In 1845 the widower married another Mount Holyoke graduate, and she died in West Africa two years later. But such tragedy did little to diminish Mount Holyoke's enthusiasm for foreign missions. When Mary died in 1849, 35 of her young women had served in this cause. And the interest continued; by 1887, 261 of the 565 women working under the auspices of the American Board were from Mount Holyoke. Until mid-century, foreign missionaries included those to the Cherokee and Choctaw Indians. Mary, by the way, left most of her personal estate to the ABCFM. Amherst's Edward Hitchcock, who as we have seen, knew Mary well, wrote this about her:

> Those who reject the doctrines of evangelical or orthodox teaching will, of course, regard her tenacious adherence to them and decided inculcation of them as unhappy defects, which more light would have removed. So those who regard revivals of religion as of doubtful utility, or the results of fanaticism, and those who suppose it indelicate for a teacher to

make individual appeals to her pupils respecting personal religion, will regard the whole system of means adopted by this lady as improper.

Hitchcock also contended that "If we look back upon the whole life of Miss Lyon, we can hardly fail to see that the controlling influence of Christian benevolence was the grand secret of her extraordinary success."

This benevolence manifested itself in many ways, most importantly perhaps in the founding of Mount Holyoke for women who were not affluent. In her personal life Mary was most generous. When her widowed sister Lovinia was sent to a mental institution, Mary paid the bills and saw to it that the children were well placed. Many of her nieces and nephews were educated through her largesse; these included Aaron Lyon who attended Oberlin College and and Abigail Moore who went to Ipswich and later to Mount Holyoke—first as a student and later as Mary's right hand. Mary also made monetary contributions to Mount Holyoke, especially in the 1830s when money was so scarce.

The fact that Mount Holyoke Seminary endured is a testament not only to Mary's foresight, but to her astute judgment of persons and to her organizational and financial abilities. She understood that it was essential for the institution to continue to prosper without her, and directed her energies to that end. Perhaps that was one reason why she asked people not to refer to Mount Holyoke as "Miss Lyon's Seminary."

Mary was so single-minded about improving women's education that she appears to have had little interest in feminism. In 1836 she wrote to Catherine Beecher:

> You speak of the importance of raising the compensation of teachers. In a list of motives for teaching, I should place first the great motive, which cannot be understood by the natural heart, Love thy neighbor as thyself. On this list, though not second in rank, I have been accustomed to place pecuniary considerations. I am inclined to the opinion that this should fall lower on the list of motives to be presented to the ladies than to gentlemen, and this is more in accordance with the system of divine government. Let us cheerfully make all the concessions, where God had designed a difference in the situation of the sexes, such as woman's retiring from public stations, being generally dependent on the other sex for pecuniary support, etc.

She added, "O that we may plead constantly for her religious privileges, for equal facilities for the improvement of her talents, and for the privilege of using all her talents to do good!"

Mary seems to have disapproved of the abolitionists. In the 1840s, as the antislavery cause came more into focus in New England, some church members felt strongly that funds should be directed toward this rather than foreign missions. Mary did not agree. Some of her sentiments are expressed in her publication entitled A *Missionary Offering*. In 1845 a man named Jefferson Church tried to persuade her to accept black students at Mount Holyoke. There is indirect evidence that the trustees declined to do so. Mary died before the Compromise of 1850 with its objectionable Fugitive Slave Law that changed the thinking of many Northerners; perhaps it would have changed her attitude.

Mary Lyon and Emma Willard differed in some personal characteristics. Mary was more self-effacing and probably less egotistic than Emma, probably also less vain and less interested in her appearance. She certainly lived more modestly and expected those around her to do the same. Emma was elegant, Mary plain. Jill Kerr Conway, when president of Smith College, pointed out that while Emma was inspired by patriotism, Mary was inspired by the Methodist doctrine of the possibility of the perfection of society and perfection of the individual spirit. It is interesting that both women, though deeply religious, realized the importance of science and strived to see it taught well.

Mount Holyoke alumnae are known throughout the world, while such colleges as Mills, Lake Erie and Western, as well as several foreign institutions, were founded on Mount Holyoke principles. Mary Lyon predicted correctly when she wrote to Zilpah in 1836: "This will be an era in female education. The work will not stop with this institution. This enterprise may have to struggle through embarrassments for years, but its influence will be felt."

One hundred and fifty years after the founding of Mount Holyoke College a two-cent stamp was issued in honor of Mary Lyon.

Harriet Beecher Stowe
Uncle Tom's Cabin

"As Columbus sought an old continent and discovered a new one, so Harriet Beecher Stowe meant to write an argument on an old theme and succeeded in writing an immortal classic." So wrote scholar and critic William Lyon Phelps about *Uncle Tom's Cabin*. This chapter looks at the author and her enduring monument.

Harriet Elizabeth Beecher was born on June 14, 1811, in Litchfield, Connecticut, the seventh child of Lyman and Roxanna (Foote) Beecher. Her father was a Congregational minister, educated at Yale, who became a leading cleric in the United States. A foe of dueling, Catholicism and Unitarianism, he was later a leading advocate of temperance. Roxanna was educated, gentle and loved by many. Harriet was devoted to her memory but could not have known her mother well, for Roxanna died of tuberculosis (after bearing nine children in 17 years) when Harriet was four. The next year, Lyman married Harriet Porter of Portland, Maine, and that union produced four more children.

Although she had a stepmother, Catherine Beecher, Harriet's oldest sister, seems to have mothered her. Lyman appears to have been a loving father. In his family, religion was the keynote. In time his seven sons would enter the ministry; one of them, Henry Ward Beecher, would be recognized as the foremost preacher of his day. Harriet's belief that all men were children of God undoubtedly influenced her feelings about men holding other men in bondage. However, her generation came to worship a loving God rather than the Puritans' god of wrath to whom their fathers bowed.

Though small, Litchfield was nevertheless a center of learning and culture. It had a law school and also Miss Pierce's school, which we noted earlier as one of the better female academies. Harriet was enrolled at Miss Pierce's between the years 1819–24. But before that, it was apparent that she was a good student. According to a letter written by her father, "Hattie is a genius. I would give a hundred dollars if she was a boy. She is as odd as she is intelligent and studious." Her formal schooling, heavily weighted in religion, was supplemented by reading and her father's sermons and discussions; in fact, from him she learned the art of logical and persuasive argument, for which he was famous.

Harriet Beecher Stowe—1852. Courtesy Stowe-Day Foundation.

Catherine opened her Hartford Female Seminary in 1823, and the following year Harriet went there to study for the next three years. An arrangement was worked out so that she lived in the home of a family whose daughter in turn lived with the Beechers while she was attending Miss Pierce's school.

In 1826 Lyman Beecher left Litchfield to become minister at the Hanover Street Church in Boston. Harriet sometimes visited the family home, but all her life seemed to regard her stepmother as cold. Now a grown woman, the future author was petite in stature and rather plain, somewhat engaging and endowed with a sense of humor. She spent a good part of the next three years as a teacher at Catherine's school. At various times she taught Latin, rhetoric and composition. By 1828 there was a hint of her destiny when she wrote to her brother Edward: ". . . I do not mean to live in vain. He has given me talents, and I will lay them at his feet, well satisfied if He will accept them."

During her adolescent years Harriet experienced religious doubts, and these caused her much anguish. She eventually worked out her faith, expressing it in the beautiful hymn "Still, Still with Thee." Clearly religion was the cornerstone of her life, though her beliefs may have differed from her father's.

Still, Still with Thee

Still, still with Thee, when purple morning breaketh,
    When the bird waketh and the shadows flee;
Fairer than morning, lov'lier than the daylight,
    Dawns the sweet consciousness, *I am with Thee!*

Alone with Thee! amid the mustic shadows,
    The solemn hush of nature newly born;
Alone with Thee in breathless adoration,
    In the calm dew and freshness of the morn.

As in the dawning, o'er the waveless ocean,
    The image of the morning star doth rest.
So, in this stillness, Thou beholdest only
    Thine image in the waters of my breast.

Still, still with Thee! As to each new-born morning
    A fresh and solemn splendor still is given,
So doth this blessed consciousness, awaking,
    Breathe each new day nearness to Thee and heaven.

When sinks the soul, subdued by soil, to slumber,
    Its closing eye looks up to Thee in prayer,
Sweet the repose beneath Thy wings o'ershading,
    But sweeter still to wake and find Thee there.

So shall it be at last, in that bright morning,
    When the soul waketh, and life's shadows flee;
Oh! in that hour, fairer than daylight dawning,
    Shall rise the glorious thought—*I am with thee!*

    —from *A Treasure of Hymns*
    by Amos R. Wells, 1914.

After serving six years in Boston, Lyman Beecher decided it was time for him and his progeny to proselyte what was then the West. He wrote to Catherine, always a favorite with him, about the importance of educating the young generation "in which Catholics and infidels have got the start on us." In 1832 most of the Beecher family moved to Cincinnati, "The London of the West." Here Beecher had been appointed president of a new institution, Lane Theological Seminary. He was also pastor of the Second Presbyterian Church. (Congregationalism and Presbyterianism were apparently so similar that there was no difficulty in changing from one to the other.) Catherine started another school, and Harriet taught here until late 1835.

In Connecticut and Massachusetts most people had little contact with blacks and less with slavery. True, Harriet had heard about an aunt who married a planter and subsequently was horrified to find when she reached the West Indies that he was the father of several mulatto children. But in Cincinnati the young teacher would learn more about race relations. The city was a center of commerce in a free state, but much of its trade was with the South and many of the inhabitants had proslavery leanings. Just across the Ohio River was Kentucky, where slavery was legal, and it was not unusual for slaves to escape from their masters by fleeing across the Ohio. Also, constantly passing through were vessels bound down river to sell their cargoes of men, women and children. Announcements offering rewards for escaped slaves were commonplace. Besides fugitive slaves there were about 2500 free Negroes in the city. During the 18 years she lived in Cincinnati, Harriet certainly came to realize the evils of slavery. She was once invited by a fellow-teacher to visit a Kentucky plantation some 60 miles from Cincinnati. Though she said very little about what she saw, she later depicted much of it in *Uncle Tom*.

Harriet was a child when the Compromise of 1820 was reached. Missouri was admitted to the Union as a slave state with the agreement that the rest of the territory of the Louisiana Purchase, north of 36° 30′, was to be free. This was an effort by the North to check the spread of slavery in the developing nation.

Antislavery forces were mainly of two persuasions. The abolitionists, led by William Lloyd Garrison of Massachusetts, stood uncompromisingly for immediate emancipation of all held in bondage. Colonizationists wished to free Negroes and then send them to Africa or elsewhere. Some antislavery people who were beginning to fear a civil war felt that the abolitionists were too reckless. Neither abolitionists nor colonizationists offered practical means for accomplishing their objectives. Many abolitionists were former colonizationists whose views had become more advanced. In general those who believed in the equality of the races believed that free Negroes should remain here. Both groups harbored racists, but it should be realized that at the time, very little was known about genetics, and people sincerely believed in the superiority of the white race.

Almost immediately Lane became embroiled in the abolitionism vs. colonization issue. The prime mover was Theodore Dwight Weld. Weld had been converted by evangelist Charles Grandison Finney and had come to Lane to study theology. Though technically a student, he was 30 and endowed with leadership ability and an unusual gift for oratory. As a general agent for a society that promoted manual labor in literary institutions, he had traveled in the South and seen slavery firsthand. He became committed to abolitionism and was determined to make Lane a center for abolitionist activities. Many of the students were, like him, older than usual and recently converted by Finney. Weld believed wholeheartedly in the equality of the races and mingled freely with the blacks of Cincinnati. Though most of the Lane trustees were colonizationists, and Beecher seems to have believed that moral persuasion of the planters would bring about emancipation, Weld set out to convert the student body to his way of thinking. In 1834 the so-called Lane debate explored over a period of several evenings whether immediatism or colonization should prevail. Weld and his followers convinced many, and there was an overwhelming vote for immediatism.

But the young leader believed in works, not just words, and Lane students decided to "elevate the colored population of Cincinnati." This they did by teaching and lecturing and also visiting the homes of free Negroes. During the summer they invited some black girls to picnic on grounds belonging to the seminary. A few members of Cincinnati's press became alarmed, as did the trustees, some of whom did business in the South. With Beecher away on a fund-raising trip, the board in August declared that slavery was not a subject for immature minds, and forbade any societies, public statements or discussions not related to theology. Things went from bad to worse — so much so that Beecher could not undo the damage when he returned. The result of the whole affair was that 51 of the students withdrew from the institution. Many transferred to Oberlin College. From then on it was downhill for Lane.

Weld did not go to Oberlin with the dissenting theologs. He continued his abolitionist activities as an agent of the American Anti-Slavery Society, training others in his successful techniques. In 1839 he published anonymously his powerful *Slavery As It Is,* some of which Harriet would use as basic material for *Uncle Tom's Cabin.* Weld certainly approached Garrison in his effectiveness in the abolitionist movement.

If Harriet had been unaware of the growing conflict over slavery, the departure of the students must have impressed her with the seriousness of the situation as early as the 1830's.

In 1833, at Catherine's suggestion, Harriet wrote a children's geography book. Published by Corey, Webster and Fairbanks, it sold very well and was Harriet's first publication. Her literary aspirations were further stimulated by the Semi-Colon Club. This had been organized by her maternal uncle, Samuel Foote, a retired sea captain originally from Connecticut and now settled in Cincinnati. His love of novels by Scott, poetry by Byron, essays by Irving and so on had influenced Harriet when she was younger. He also claimed that certain Catholics, Jews and Turks whom he knew were just as righteous as Protestants. This viewpoint was novel to his niece and certainly foreign to her father. Now he offered his fine home for weekly meetings of the literary society. Among the members was Judge James Hall, editor of the *Western Monthly Magazine.* When Harriet read her story, *A New England Sketch,* Hall urged her to submit it to a contest being run by his magazine. She did and won $50. This helped bolster her confidence in herself as an author and impressed her family.

During this time she became friendly with Eliza Stowe, daughter of the president of Dartmouth College. Eliza was the wife of Clavin Stowe, a leading scholar and Lane's professor of biblical literature. The friendship was short-lived, for Eliza died in the summer of 1834.

Their mutual regard for Eliza brought Harriet and the scholarly Calvin Stowe together, and they were married in 1836. A few months later Calvin sailed for Europe to buy books for Lane and also to study public education. The Ohio state government was behind the latter movement, for the push for public schools had begun. Harriet did not accompany him, because she was pregnant. Her brother Henry was temporary editor of the *Cincinnati Journal and Western Luminary,* and she was helping him.

That summer Harriet again witnessed violence in Cincinnati. A few months before, a street fight between a black and a white boy had touched off a race riot, with the state militia being called out. The current action revolved around James Birney. A Southerner converted to abolitionism by Weld, Birney published an abolitionist paper named the *Philanthropist.* While Southern buyers and planters were visiting the city on business, a mob damaged the press and type. Harriet mentioned in a letter to her husband that most respectable citizens overlooked the outrage. For the *Journal* she wrote an editorial under a pen name in defense of freedom of speech and the press, not abolitionism. To Calvin she wrote, ". . . I can easily see how such proceedings may make converts to abolitionism, for already my sympathies are strongly enlisted for Mr. Birney."

The damage repaired, Birney published the next edition of his unpopular weekly. But the violence continued; Birney was warned to leave town and when he refused a mob sought him. Fortunately they did not find him. But in the end his press, owned by a courageous Quaker printer, was smashed and thrown into the river. The mob's last act was to set afire some Negro shacks.

Birney gave up the editorship but not his commitment to the cause. Unlike Garrison, he believed in political action, and founded the Liberty Party. He was its candidate for president in 1840 and again in 1844. Incidentally, his Cincinnati assistant editor was Dr. Gamaliel Bailey, a young surgeon who would later edit the Washington-based abolitionist weekly that first published *Uncle Tom* in serial form.

The Birney affair had a significant effect on Harriet. Her son Charles quoted her as saying:

> I saw for the first time clearly that the institution of slavery was incapable of defence and that it was for this reason that its supporters were compelled to resort to mob-violence . . . [I] was confident that it was doomed, and that it would go, but how or when I could not picture to myself. That summer and fall opened my eyes to the real nature of slavery as they had never been opened before.

In 1838 the Stowes became the parents of a set of girl twins. By 1849 there were six children. The family lived in genteel poverty and Harriet tried to supplant Calvin's salary, sometimes not paid in full because of financial difficulties at Lane, by writing pieces for newspapers and magazines.

She had some success and by 1843 Harper Brothers had published *The Mayflower*, a series of New England sketches. Calvin encouraged her. Here is part of a letter to her: "My dear, you must be a literary woman. It is so written in the book of fate . . . Drop the E. out of your name. It only encumbers it and interferes with the flow and euphony. Write yourself fully and always Harriet Beecher Stowe. . . ."

A New Englander at heart, Harriet did not care for Cincinnati. In June 1845, she wrote to Calvin: "I am sick of the smell of sour milk, and sour meat, and sour everything, and then the clothes *will* not dry . . . and everything smells mouldy; and altogether I feel as if I never wanted to eat again."

As the years went by, cholera epidemics, race riots and hot weather made her long more and more for New England.

She sometimes hired former slaves for domestic work, and they talked to her about their lives in bondage. Here she describes in a letter the life of one of them called Eliza Buck:

> She had lived through the whole sad story of a Virginia-raised slave's life. In her youth she must have been a very handsome mulatto girl. Her voice was sweet & her manners refined and agreeable. She was raised in a good family, as nurse & sempstress. When the family became embarrassed, she was suddenly sold on to a plantation in Louisiana . . . She has told me of scenes on the Louisiana plantations & how she has often been out in the night by stealth, ministering to poor slaves, who had been mangled & lacerated by the whip. Thence she was sold again into Kentucky, and her last Master was the father of all her children.

At one time Harriet ran a small private school which she allowed black children to attend. It turned out that one of them, a little boy, was not free, as she had supposed, but was about to be sold to settle the affairs of a Kentucky estate. The frantic mother appealed to Harriet for help, and through neighborhood subscription the child's freedom was bought. More than once the Stowes sheltered fugitive slaves, and once her husband and brother helped a hunted woman escape by night to a farm outside the city.

Cincinnati's racial clashes continued. During the summer of 1849, the Stowes' youngest child, not yet two, died from cholera. After the publication of *Uncle Tom's Cabin*, Harriet wrote this in a letter: "It was at his dying bed and at his grave that I learned what a poor slave must feel when her child is torn away from her . . . I allude to this here because I have often felt that much that is in that book had its roots in the awful scenes and bitter sorrows of that summer." For years Calvin Stowe had felt he was worth more than Lane could afford to pay him. Nevertheless he remained there because of his loyalty to Dr. Beecher. However, when Bowdoin College in Brunswick, Maine, offered him a position as Collings Professor of Natural and Revealed Religion, he accepted.

The year 1850 saw the Stowes in Brunswick. Harriet had given birth to another child soon after leaving Cincinnati. She was happy to be back in New England, but she could not ignore the mounting tension over slavery as the South tried to extend the institution into new territories and the North fought to contain it. One of the Bowdoin professors was sure that blood would be spilled before the issue was resolved.

Texas had been admitted to the Union as a slave state, California as free. The status of the territories of New Mexico and Utah would be worked out when they applied for statehood. To appease the South, Congress passed more stringent legislation relating to fugitive slaves. It was now illegal for citizens in free states to obstruct the return of escaped slaves to their owners; in fact, they were supposed to aid the federal marshals and their deputies. An apprehended black had no access to a jury trial, so free Negroes were liable to be returned to bondage. (There had been a federal fugitive slave law since 1793, but this was generally disregarded in the North.) The abolitionists were infuriated at this new statute.

Harriet was certainly antislavery, but she had never allied herself with the militant abolitionists. Now the fugitive slave legislation triggered her to action. Her brother Edward and his wife had long been abolitionists, and his wife Isabella wrote: "Hattie, if I could use a pen as you can, I would write something that will make this whole nation feel what an accursed thing slavery is."

Harriet's reply was, "As long as the baby sleeps with me nights I can't do much at any thing — but I shall do it at last. I shall write that thing if I live . . . ."

She began "the thing" a few months later. To Dr. Bailey, now the editor of the *National Era,* she wrote:

> I am at present occupied upon a story which will be much longer than any I have written, embracing a series of sketches which give the lights and shadows of the "patriarchial institution," written either from observation, incidents which have occurred in the sphere of my personal observation, or in the knowledge of my friends. I shall show the *best side* of the thing, and something *faintly approaching the worst.*

> My vocation is simply that of a painter, and my object will be to hold up in the most lifelike and graphic manner possible Slavery, its reverses, changes, and the negro character, which I have had ample opportunities for studying. There is no arguing with *pictures,* and everyone is impressed by them. . . .

After coping with the daily demands of her large family, Harriet had little time or energy to write. To add to her obligations, Dr. Beecher, now 75, along with his third wife and one of his stepdaughters, paid a visit. His current interest was preparing his theological views for publication, and he worked at that, little suspecting that his daughter's work in progress would far outshine his.

Harriet had originally projected a three- or four-part story, but she found that it was getting longer and longer as everything she had seen or read or heard about slavery came to mind. Fortunately Catherine took over management of the Stowe household for a year and freed her sister to finish "the thing," which ultimately contained 44 chapters.

From the beginning the readers loved *Uncle Tom.* There were protests when Harriet missed a deadline. When the magazine suggested that the story could be finished quickly with a summary, the following letter was sent to the editor:

> Please signify to Mrs. Stowe that it will be quite agreeable to the wishes of the many readers of the Era for her *not to hurry through* "Uncle Tom." We don't get sleepy reading it. Having resided many years among slaves and being familiar with their habits, thoughts, feelings and language, I have not been able to detect a single mistake in her story in any of these respects — 'tis perfect in its way — will do great good.

Following the serialized version, the story appeared in book form in 1852 as *Uncle Tom's Cabin: or, Life among the Lowly.* J.P. Jewett had

135,000 SETS, 270,000 VOLUMES SOLD.

UNCLE TOM'S CABIN

FOR SALE HERE.

AN EDITION FOR THE MILLION, COMPLETE IN 1 Vol., PRICE 37 1-2 CENTS.
" " IN GERMAN, IN 1 Vol., PRICE 50 CENTS.
" " IN 2 Vols., CLOTH, 6 PLATES, PRICE $1.50.
SUPERB ILLUSTRATED EDITION, IN 1 Vol., WITH 153 ENGRAVINGS,
PRICES FROM $2.50 TO $5.00.

The Greatest Book of the Age.

An advertisement for *Uncle Tom's Cabin*. Courtesy Stowe-Day Foundation.

published it at the suggestion of his wife, who had been following it in the *Era*. It was an immediate success — an unprecedented bestseller in the United States and especially in Britain. It is still in print and has been translated into about 30 languages.

Very soon *Uncle Tom* plays emerged and remained popular well into the twentieth century. Harriet did not approve of the theater and never sanctioned the use of *Uncle Tom's Cabin* for performance. However, there were many dramatizations — some good and some very far from representing the original.

Uncle Tom's Cabin is the story of Tom, a trusted Negro slave who lives on a Kentucky plantation, and of the light-skinned Eliza and George Harris, who have a young child named Harry. Due to straited circumstances of his kind master, Tom is sold to a slave trader. His wife, Chloe, and their children left behind, he is bought by Augustine St. Clare of New Orleans. Here he is treated well and becomes a favorite of St. Clare's young daughter Eva. When Eliza learns that her little Harry is also to be sold, she runs away, taking him with her. Holding him in her arms, she jumps across the ice floes of the melting Ohio River, leaving her pursuers on the Kentucky side. She arrives safely on the Ohio side and is taken to the home of a Quaker family. There she is joined by her husband, George, who has also managed to escape from his master (who is different from Eliza's). The Harrises finally reach Canada, where they are free. In time George gets a university education and takes his family to Liberia. There are bad times ahead for Tom; when St. Clare meets sudden death, his loyal slave is sold to the brutal Simon Legree, who owns a cotton plantation in a wild, remote spot some distance from the Red River. Legree sneers at Tom's steadfast faith in God and is infuriated at his indifference to Legree's threats. (The slave replied, "Ye may whip me, starve me, burn me, — it'll only send me sooner where I want to go.") When Tom refuses to flog a woman slave, as his master orders, the cruel Legree has his slave beaten to death. As Tom is dying, the son of his former Kentucky master arrives to take him back to his family; Chloe had been allowed to work out to earn money to purchase her husband's freedom. But it is too late.

The foregoing is only a brief outline of the plot. The book is full of pathos, humor and colorful characters such as Topsy, the droll little slave girl whom St. Clare bought for his circumspect cousin Ophelia to improve with a New England upbringing. The reader meets Cassie, the beautiful and tragic slave whose children have been sold; Mrs. Bird, the Ohio senator's wife who knows that her husband, despite what he says, will take fugitive slaves — and others.

Years of religious experience had convinced Harriet that owning human beings was a sin and must cease. Her story line made the evils of slavery crystal clear, but being the daughter of Lyman Beecher, she reinforced it with religious and logical arguments not unlike sermons. The abolitionists had written scores of tracts presenting facts and figures on slavery. *Uncle Tom's Cabin* was antislavery propaganda, but it was fiction that depicted blacks so vividly that whites began to understand the Negroes' plight. White mothers could identify with Eliza as she fled to save her child from being sold; white men could see black Tom as a real person, sustained by the promise of the same Bible so familiar to them. It is true that the slave was seen through white eyes, but this is important because the power structure lay in white hands, not black. By making an imaginative and emotional appeal to the conscience of the North, the book did much to abolish slavery, though not without a terrible civil war. Churchill in *A History of the English-Speaking Peoples* termed it "the herald of the storm."

Ironically, Harriet had hoped to persuade the South that slavery was sinful; she was attacking the system rather than individuals. While abolitionist tracts tended to paint slaveholders as completely evil, Harriet presented a balanced picture. For instance, she portrayed some humane and lovable Southerners, while Simon Legree was a native Vermonter. But she failed to move the South; Southerners soon realized the power of the novel and banned it.

Over the years the book has been harshly criticized. Literary critics have complained about its preaching and plot structure. With regard to its authenticity, a distinguished scholar wrote: "Much of the book is true, considered as a body of isolated facts. As a whole, it is a wholesale lie; since it seeks, from instances which are of anomalous and occasional occurrence only, to establish general conditions and conclusions for a people." And this sentiment is echoed by others.

Many blacks have resented Harriet's paternalistic treatment of the Negro and especially that she had George Harris decide to take his family to Africa. Some of them believe she did immeasurable harm by reinforcing false stereotypes. As late as the 1980s, Station WGBH of Boston produced for *Spider's Web* a seven-part drama of *Uncle Tom's Cabin* with James Earl Jones playing the part of Tom. However, members of the local black community felt very strongly that the book was racist and should not be aired. WGBH management honored their conviction by agreeing that this production would not be aired as part of this series for young adults. Showtime's 1987 full-length, sound movie version of the novel was well received by educators.

The importance of *Uncle Tom* lies in its social impact rather than its literary worth. Obviously considerable literary skill was needed to move people as Harriet's book did. Novelist George Sand noted that it had its faults only in terms of conventional rules of art and said of those who

Drawing made for *Spider's Web* radio show. Courtesy Elliott Banfield.

criticized this aspect, ". . . look well to see if their eyes are dry while reading this or that chapter." Dickens had criticism but nevertheless termed the book "a noble work." Edmund Wilson, considered one of the twentieth century's most important literary and social critics, wrote in the *New Yorker*, "If you have never read it, you should."

Uncle Tom brought Harriet fame and fortune. As one of the most prominent women in the United States, she visited Lincoln at the White House to assure herself that the Emancipation Proclamation would take effect on January 1, 1863, even if the South returned to the Union. It is said that on meeting Harriet, the president remarked, "So this is the little lady who made this big war."

In 1853, when two Glasgow antislavery societies invited the Stowes to visit England and Scotland with all expenses paid, Harriet was lionized by the public from all walks of life. Few persons have ever received such acclaim.

After Bowdoin, Calvin had a professorship at Andover Theological Seminary in Massachusetts for 11 years. When he retired the Stowes settled in Hartford, Connecticut. Harriet also purchased property in Mandarin, Florida, where they spent much time. Fame did not spare Harriet grief; the Stowes lost one son in a drowning accident and another to alcoholism. But their marriage seems to have been a good one.

A Key to Uncle Tom's Cabin: Presenting the Original Facts and Documents upon Which the Story Is Founded was published in 1853. In this factual work Harriet attempted to explain the authenticity of *Uncle Tom*, leaning heavily on Weld's book. She continued to produce literary works. *Dred: A Tale of the Great Dismal Swamp*, published in 1856, was another antislavery novel. Other titles included *The Minister's Wooing, Pink and White Tyranny: A Society Novel, Palmetto Leaves* and *Poganuc People: Their Loves and Lives*. Some consider her *Oldtown Folks* (1869) and *Oldtown Fireside Stories* (1872) significant contributions to American literature. However, it is generally agreed that none of these books approaches *Uncle Tom*.

Harriet did not ally herself with the feminists. Her preoccupation with religion continued to influence most of the facets of her life. She was somewhat like her father in believing that reform could be brought about through prayer and persuasion.

Harriet Beecher Stowe died in 1896, ten years after her husband. During the last seven years of her life, her faculties failed. She was elected to the Hall of Fame for Great Americans in 1910. It would please her to know that *Uncle Tom's Cabin* is discussed in *Books That Changed America*, written by Robert Downs, and that *The Literary History of the United States* describes it as "the most influential novel of all history."

Julia Ward Howe
"Battle Hymn of the Republic"

"She embodied that trait more essential than any other in the makeup of the men and women of the Republic — the valor of righteousness," wrote Theodore Roosevelt, referring to Julia Ward Howe. During her 91 years, this woman was wife, mother, poet, abolitionist, author, feminist, lecturer, humanitarian, pacifist and recipient of three honorary degrees. But her enduring monument is "Battle Hymn of the Republic."

Julia was born in New York City in 1819. Her ancestors on both sides had fought in the War of Independence. Her father, Samuel Ward, was a wealthy banker and philanthropist. Julia Rush Cutler Ward, his wife, had died when Julia was five. Mrs. Cutler, who had battled tuberculosis for 11 years and was finally downed by puerperal fever, probably had little direct influence on her daughter; however, she did write poetry, and perhaps this encouraged the girl who would write one of America's best loved hymns.

Mr. Ward was devastated by the death of his young wife. Turning to religion, he sought to protect his six children from "the dissipations of fashionable society." The boys were sent to boarding school, and a devoted aunt moved into the household to help raise her sister's daughters. She remained there long after she married and had a family of her own.

Although the Ward girls were kept at home more than they cared to be, they were loved and indulged. They spent their summers in Newport, Rhode Island, and their father did not stint on their education. At first they were instructed by nursery governesses and masters who even taught them foreign languages, dancing and music. By the time Julia was nine, she was allowed to attend private neighborhood schools for the next seven years or so. She must have had a low opinion of her formal education, for in old age she wrote, "I left school at the age of 16 and began thereafter to study in earnest." She apparently had been exposed to the type of female education deplored by Emma Willard and Mary Lyon.

Julia did indeed become a lifetime student. She understood Latin and spoke and wrote French, German and Italian; she had a thorough knowledge of the Bible; she became an accomplished pianist and singer with a mezzo-soprano voice. Her oldest brother, Sam, was a good scholar and in time assembled a collection of books that was available to Julia. She read George Sand, Balzac, Goethe and others. (Shelley was forbidden and Byron restricted.) Francis Marion, another brother, observed, "Much does she seem resolving over some plan for literary distinction, but this, I hope, she will lay aside when she grows older and wiser." Little did he know his sister! Sam, on the other hand, did not discourage her literary aspirations. The family had tried to interest Julia in domestic matters, but it was clear that she preferred intellectual pursuits.

In 1840 Julia's favorite brother, Henry, died from typhoid. The next summer, the Ward girls visited his fiancee in Dorchester, Massachusetts. During this stay Julia met her husband-to-be, Samuel Gridley Howe.

Howe was then 40 and his *History of the Greek Revolution* was well known publicly. A graduate of Brown University and Harvard Medical School, he had served for two years as a medical officer in the Greek forces struggling to gain independence from the Turks. Then he came home to raise money for reconstruction. Successful in this effort, he spent another two years in Greece, this time concentrating on the country's recovery. When he returned to Boston in 1831, he was appointed director of the New England Asylum of the Blind. Yet another trans–Atlantic voyage brought him to Europe in quest of materials and methods for teaching the blind. He became involved in the plight of Poles who had tried in 1830 to revolt against the Prussians. For this he was imprisoned briefly in Berlin. Fortunately his release was obtained through the efforts of an American who was in Berlin at the time.

Under Howe the Asylum (today Perkins School for the Blind) made rapid strides. By 1839 it was named Perkins Institution and located in a former hotel in South Boston. Howe lived there in the Doctor's Wing with his sister Jeanette acting as housekeeper. One of the school's most famous pupils was Laura Bridgman, deaf and blind since early childhood, to whom Howe taught communication. The doctor's major responsibility was the blind, but he was intensely interested in reform for the insane, for prisoners and for other downtrodden groups.

A trip to the South had turned Howe into an ardent abolitionist. Among his close personal friends were Charles Sumner, who as Senator from Massachusetts would stand unyielding in the fight against slavery; Horace Mann, who would bring reform and innovation to public education, and Henry Wadsworth Longfellow, the poet. Howe's daughters described Sumner as their father's "alter ego, the brother of his heart."

According to all accounts, Howe was a handsome man who liked to show off his skills as a superior horseman. He had a peculiar disdain for money, although he was not wealthy himself. Unlike Julia, he had little time or desire for a social life. His friends called him Chev since he held the title of Chevalier of the Greek Legion of Honor.

When Julia first met Howe, she was 21, vivacious and fun-loving. Small and red-haired, she wore beautiful clothes and loved parties. She also had a serious side. Cornelius Felton, professor of Greek at Harvard and friend of both Sam Ward and Chev, described her as "quite the most remarkable person I ever knew; I am astonished that all unmarried men are not piled up at her feet."

During the winter of 1842, Julia was in Boston again. She seems to have attended many parties. Dickens visited Boston that year, and Julia spoke with him. Her literary aspirations were still in the fore. By now some of her poems had appeared in the *Democratic Review*, and she had high hopes that Boston's George Ticknor would publish a collection of her poetry. But he turned her down.

A few months later, Julia and Chev met again in New York and a romance developed. The doctor neither cared for nor approved of Sam Ward, who for Julia was in loco parentis since the death of their father in 1839. Chev wrote Sam that he intended to marry Julia, at the same time stating that his salary was $3000 a year. The worldly Sam, who with an uncle made decisions about Julia's inheritance, regarded $3000 as "a mere pittance." Francis Marion referred to Howe as "that confounded bit of New England granite." But the wedding date was already set.

Howe, Sumner, Longfellow and Professor Felton sailed from Boston for New York to attend the wedding. There were legal and financial matters to attend to, and immediately complications arose. Since Julia was an heiress, her uncle and brother wanted to insure that she remain independently wealthy. They proposed in an "ante-nuptial agreement" that her assets be put into a trust fund to be administered by them.

Sumner, the best man and legal advisor to Howe, contended that it would be demeaning for his friend to sign away his conjugal rights, and urged him to take what he was legally entitled to. When Chev claimed he did not know Julia was wealthy, her uncle was convinced that Howe was a fortune hunter. Howe perhaps would have preferred a poor bride, but since Julia had money, he intended to be in charge of it, as was the custom.

Finally they reached a compromise: Julia's property would remain in trust; $3000 of the income would be paid annually to her and $10,000 to Howe on demand to furnish a house. It was also agreed that the bride would be known as Julia Ward Howe rather than Mrs. Samuel Gridley Howe.

The wedding took place at the home of Julia's uncle on April 26, 1843. The bride's dress of fine white muslin with lace inserts, her lace stole and net veil, as well as her white satin shoes can be seen today in the Smithsonian Institution. The groom wore a blue broadcloth coat with brass buttons, a white brocade vest and tan pants. According to Longfellow, "at supper, her [Julia's] natural roguery broke out, and seeing Sumner bend over, and

Julia Ward Howe. Engraving by C.A. Powell after a photo by J.J. Hawes. Courtesy Library of Congress.

utterly engaged in talking to a lady, she could not help slipping two of their silver spoons into his pockets." Sumner was not noted for his sense of humor, and he probably did not appreciate the laughter when the spoons were discovered in his possession.

The wedding trip was an extended visit to Europe. The newlyweds sailed from Boston on a Cunard Line steamer. Horace Mann and his bride, Mary Peabody (sister-in-law of Nathaniel Hawthorne), were aboard, as was Annie Ward, Julia's 17-year-old sister. Annie was to be chaperoned by the Howes, and the two couples would stay at the same lodgings in London.

Through the Ward family and Chev's friends, the Howes did not lack letters of introduction. Dickens had a high regard for Howe and took him to visit various government institutions as well as the slums. The Howes met Carlyle, Wordsworth and many other celebrities and non-celebrities and were able to attend cultural events. They managed to visit various parts of the British Isles and the continent before settling in Rome for the winter. Julia's letters to her sister Louisa and Chev's to Sumner described their observations and feelings. Both were appalled at the poverty they saw in Ireland.

There was great poverty in Rome too. Chev visited public institutions that were "misnamed charitable." Julia wrote poetry during this period. She was pregnant and at times depressed, apparently believing she would die in childbirth.

In December Louisa Ward joined her sisters, much to their delight. It was in Rome that Julia met Chev's friend Theodore Parker, the liberal Unitarian clergyman from Boston. He was to be her confidant and counselor for many years. Among other Americans in Rome that year was Thomas Crawford, a rising young sculptor who would marry Louisa. Howe and Mann believed in phrenology, the pseudoscience based on the belief that the conformation of the skull is indicative of mental faculties and character traits. Crawford, who had studied human anatomy, pooh-poohed this idea. But Howe grew to like Crawford, despite the latter's unorthodox view on cranial bumps.

March marked the arrival of Julia Romano Howe. A few days after her birth, Chev wrote to Sumner:

> Only a year ago Julia was a New York belle . . . To see her watching with eager, anxious eyes every moment of her offspring, to witness her entire self-forgetfulness and the total absorption of her nature in this new object of love, is to have a fresh revelation of the strength and beauty of a woman's character, and new proof of their superiority even in what most ennobles humanity—love of others.

Julia would have more children, but being a wife and mother would never satisfy her. Howe, in company with most men of his era, believed strongly that husband, family and home should be the complete focus of his wife's endeavors. Julia's thinking was much more in line with that of today's feminist, and their diverse philosophies would cause strife in their marriage.

The Howes and Wards returned home via England. When Florence Nightingale, then 24, learned that Samuel Gridley Howe was in the vicinity, she asked her parents to invite Chev and his wife to the Nightingale home. Here the woman who would revolutionize nursing asked the doctor's advice on whether she should devote her life to charitable work in hospitals and other health care facilities. He encouraged her to go ahead. He also knew and admired Dorothea Dix, who was working in the United States to improve conditions of the insane. Later in life, Julia felt that since her husband approved of the activities of these two young women, it was unfair for him not to encourage her literary and public career. She apparently failed to grasp that his approval of such pursuits extended only to *single* women.

Julia's life in South Boston was a far cry from her New York existence. She found herself surrounded by blind and other handicapped persons, from whom she at first shrank. In time she overcame her feelings and became a sincere friend to those at the Institution. Until now she had never had to worry about household duties. She could have maids, but she would have to learn how to direct them. Since Chev liked to have Sumner and other close men friends to dinner frequently, Julia purchased a copy of Catherine Beecher's cookbook and did her best. By 1847 she was able to report to Louisa that at a dinner for these men she served soup, salmon, sweetbreads, roast lamb and pigeon with green peas, potatoes, spinach and salad. Then there were pudding and blancmange, then strawberries, pineapple and ice cream.

In 1845 Florence (named for Florence Nightingale) was born. That year Julia wrote to Louisa: "Sumner has been dining with us, and he and Chev have been pitying unmarried women. Oh, my friends, thought I, if you could only have one baby, you would change your tune...."

The doctor's work occupied most of his time. Here in a letter to Annie, Julia gave a glimpse of the situation: "I went alone, Chev being philan-thropically engaged—party being over, I called for him at Mr. Mann's, but they were so happy over their report that they concluded to make a night of it, and I came home alone. Chev returned at one, quite intoxicated with benevolence...."

She sang to her baby:

> Rero, rero, riddlety rad,
> This morning my baby caught sight of her Dad.
> Quoth she, "Oh, Daddy, where have you been?"
> "With Mann and Sumner a-putting down sin!"

In short, Julia seems to have felt isolated in South Boston. By 1846 the Howes had moved into a house of their own, close to the Institution. Jeanette stayed on at Perkins, and according to two of his daughters, the doctor often moved his family back there for weeks or months. Also, the Howes frequently spent the winters in Boston proper. In a letter written in 1847 to Louisa, Julia states that she is depressed. She recounts all her blessings, but adds:

> ...the soul whose desires are not fixed upon the unattainable is dead even while it liveth, and ... I am glad, in the midst of all my comforts, to feel myself a pilgrim in pursuit of something that is neither house nor lands, nor children, nor health. What that something is I scarce know. Sometimes it seems to me one thing and sometimes another.

A little later, writing to Annie, she dwells less on herself and underlines one of her husband's reform interests. It is noteworthy because it presages the outstanding oratorical ability that would make Charles Sumner so effective in the Senate.

> Boston has been in great excitement at the public debates on the Prison Discipline Society, which have been intensely interesting. Chev and Sumner have each spoken twice, in behalf of the Philadelphia system, and against the course of the Society. They have been furiously attacked by the opposite party. Chev's second speech drew tears from my eyes, and was very beautiful. Both of Sumner's have been fine, but the last, delivered last evening, was *masterly*. I never listened to anything with more intense interest,—he held the audience breathless for two hours and a half.

By 1850 there were two more Howe children: Henry Marion, named for his two dead maternal uncles, and Laura, whose namesake was Chev's most famous pupil.

Julia's inheritance had also become a problem because of Chev's dislike for Sam Ward, who was in charge of her investments. To Julia's uncle the doctor wrote: "If Julia's income were the equal of John Jacob Astor's, and I could have it by submitting to be advised and tutored by Mr. Samuel Ward, I would reject it; I prefer my independence." Sam resigned his trusteeship in 1847 when the Ward banking firm failed. At this point Chev recovered Julia's real estate holdings, investing them in Boston. Earlier he had persuaded his wife to sign over to him her yearly allowance of $3000. At first he periodically returned it to Sam Ward, then later agreed to accept it. But he, not Julia, decided how it was to be spent.

As the marriage foundered, Julia immersed herself more and more in study, and religion gave her great comfort. She also derived enjoyment from gatherings of such congenial people as those she met at the home of Theodore Parker.

Louisa was now living in Rome with her sculptor husband, Thomas Crawford. When she invited Julia and Annie, now Mrs. John Mailliard, to visit her, Julia jumped at the opportunity. Leaving their two older children at the Perkins Institution in the care of friends, the Howes sailed for England with Henry and Laura. After a holiday in Germany with Chev, Julia and the children took a roundabout route to Rome, where they were to spend the fall and winter.

Chev returned to Boston as planned and took little Julia and Flossy home with him. Boston was seething over the recently passed fugitive slave act, and Howe would become more intensely involved in the abolitionist cause.

Rome buoyed Julia's spirits. She studied Hebrew, took singing lessons and mingled with other intellectual Americans who were abroad. One of these was Horace Binney Wallace, a bachelor who took an interest in her but also criticized her poetry and encouraged her efforts in that field. He prompted her study of philosophy, which continued throughout her life. Julia was obviously enjoying herself, but she could not stay forever.

She was back in Boston late in the summer of 1851. Fanny Longfellow wrote to her sister: "I hear she was much admired in Rome and her soirees much courted . . . How dull she will find it in South Boston—she is not satisfied with the society of husband and children and a social nature like hers requires much more, not to consume itself."

The next year saw the Longfellows and the Howes summering together in Newport. One day Chev, on horseback, discovered a country property for sale about six miles from town. Immediately realizing its possibilities, he bought it, much to delight of his family. They would spend many happy summers there.

In 1853 Howe became editor of the *Commonwealth*, a Free Soil newspaper. He allowed Julia to contribute reviews on books, lectures, plays and concerts. However, the publication was not a great success.

A few of Julia's poems had been published; in fact, Chev had even included her "Rome Beggar Boy" in a Braille book, omitting the author's name. But Julia yearned to have a volume of poetry in print. She tried Ticknor and Fields, and this time found Fields receptive. Knowing that her husband would be averse to the project, she told him nothing about it and arranged to have authorship of the work remain anonymous. Entitled *Passion Flowers*, the volume reached a third edition.

Passion Flowers appears to have made matters worse between Julia and her husband. It very soon became public knowledge that she was the author. She wrote to Annie: "The book, you see, was a blow to him, and some foolish and impertinent people have hinted that the Miller was meant for himself—and this has made him almost crazy." The Miller is a character in a poem that ends with this stanza:

> For men will woo the tempest
>   And wed to their cost,
> Then swear they took it for summer dew
>   And ah! their peace is lost!

The reader is left to judge whether this is an innocent example of Julia's sense of humor or whether Chev's anger was justified.

Howe wanted to get out of the marriage, but keep Julia Romano and Henry with him. Julia would not agree. To Annie she wrote: "Chev is as cold and indifferent to me as a man can well be. I sometimes suspect him of having relations with another woman, and regret more bitterly the sacrifice which entailed upon me these months of fatigue and suffering." At this time she was pregnant again, carrying Maud, who was born in November 1854. In 1857 Chev repeated his request, still demanding the two children. Again Julia refused to free him.

Years later, when Howe was dying, he confessed to his wife to having an affair with a woman Julia knew. Who she was is not clear; pages of Julia's diary were removed, and at Howe's dying request, correspondence between him and Julia and between him and Sumner during 1851–52 was destroyed. After Chev's death Julia found letters at Perkins Institution that her son-in-law burned for her after suggesting that she not read them.

In 1857 another collection of Julia's poems was published under the title *Words for the Hour*. It caused no great stir but doubtless brought her personal satisfaction.

The year before, she had written *The World's Own,* a play in blank verse. It was produced briefly in New York, and Ticknor and Fields printed the text. But it was not a success, perhaps because it offended Victorian morality. Julia's heroine is a peasant girl who seeks revenge on the count who seduced her. Brother Sam loved it. To Julia he wrote: "As for the attacks, smile serenely. If you talk about the affair, say you stood up for the women's rights and had in view to show how abominable our sex is and how abused yours is. . . ." But Oliver Wendell Holmes wrote: "I don't know how so quiet a blend as yourself should have such tropical flashes of passion running through your veins." Mrs. Longfellow thought "the poor doctor must feel it painfully as a thing he cannot give his daughters to read." Three of these daughters stated in their mother's biography that in the play were "passages which show that already her heart cherished the high ideal of her sex, for which her later voice was to be uplifted."

Another play, *Hippolytus,* followed *The World's Own* but was never produced, to Julia's deep disappointment.

Incidentally, Julia could be most unreasonable with editors. She once wrote to James Russell Lowell, then editor of the *Atlantic Monthly:* "What care I if you don't like my verses? Who said you could understand them? I didn't. Yet you print worse ones, your own, very likely. . . ."

As the nation grew closer to war, Chev's antislavery leanings led him to John Brown, whose abolitionist activities were focused on Kansas in 1856. According to an act that violated the provisions of the Missouri Compromise and appropriated land designed as part of an Indian reserve, the Kansas Territory was created with the provision that its people could determine whether Kansas would enter the Union as slave or free. (The Missouri Compromise spelled out that its geographical location automatically forbade slavery.) As proslavery advocates from Missouri poured into Kansas, there was also an influx of abolitionist-backed settlers. The violence that followed gave the territory the name "Bleeding Kansas." When Lawrence, an abolitionist stronghold, was sacked by proslavery people, John Brown retaliated by leading a party of six to murder in cold blood five proslavery settlers who lived on the banks of the Pottawatamie River. Guerrilla war broke out in southeastern Kansas.

Five days before the Pottawatamie massacre, Sumner, now a United States senator, had begun his famous "Crime Against Kansas" speech on behalf of abolition in that state. In it he directly attacked Senator Butler of South Carolina. Two days later in the Senate chamber, Congressman Preston Brooks, Butler's nephew, beat Sumner severely with a cane. According to one of John Brown's sons, this news triggered the murders. John was a religious fanatic whose dream was to free slaves. He apparently believed sincerely that almost anything he did could be justified if the action led to the attainment of his goal.

Early in 1857 Brown was in the East trying to obtain money and Sharps rifles for what he represented as the abolitionist cause in Kansas; it was in reality a blind for something else. It was at this time that Chev met Brown. Brown's major plan was to establish a state for Negroes in the Appalachians, and he was convinced that slaves would flee to it. He ultimately revealed his idea to a group that came to be known as the Secret Six. It included Chev and the Rev. Theodore Parker. But Brown seems to have withheld from these six his scheme to obtain arms for his followers by taking the federal arsenal at Harper's Ferry, and so he gained their support.

Julia had met John Brown and knew of his sincere concern for blacks. Although the Wards were not abolitionists, she had gradually become one. Chev had visited Kansas as an agent of the National Kansas Committee, and she was cognizant of the turmoil there. Although Sumner was able to return to the Senate in 1859, his injuries had underscored for the Howes the seriousness of the conflict behind the attack. When Brown's ill-conceived attack on Harper's Ferry failed, Julia wrote to Annie:

> No one knew of Brown's intentions but Brown himself and his handful of men. The attempt I must judge insane but the spirit *heroic*. I should be glad to be as sure of heaven as that old man may be, following right in the footsteps of the old martyrs, girding on his sword for the weak and oppressed. His death will be holy and glorious—the gallows cannot dishonor it—he will hallow it.

Several weeks later, Samuel Gridley Howe, Jr. was born. Known as Sammy, he was Julia's last child and a great favorite.

As the decade closed Julia could consider herself an accomplished writer. In 1859 she and Chev spent several months in Cuba. This excursion prompted Julia to write *A Trip to Cuba,* which came out first as a magazine serial and then in book form the next year.

Too old to fight in the Civil War, Howe was appointed a member of the United States Sanitary Commission, created on June 13, 1861. This commission was composed of civilians who would function as watch dogs of military medicine, and also mobilize public benevolence to aid the military.

In the fall of 1861 Chev and Julia visited the city of Washington, where the doctor had business on behalf of the Sanitary Commission. Julia recalled, "As we approached the city, I saw from time to time small groups of armed men seated on the ground near a fire. Dr. Howe explained to me that these were pickets [sentinels] detailed to guard the railway." This scene is immortalized in the second stanza of the "Battle Hymn."

The Army of the Potomac was camped around the capital city to insure against capture by the enemy. One day Julia with her friends the Whipples and her pastor, Rev. James Freeman Clarke of Boston, drove in a carriage to watch General McClellan review his troops at Upton's Hill in Virginia, not too far from the Confederate lines. Howe was following on horseback. The review had to be halted because of a surprise move by the Rebels. As the carriage made its way back to Washington, it was slowed by the presence of returning troops in the road. Julia wrote: "To beguile the rather tedious drive, we sang from time to time snatches of the Army songs so popular at that time, concluding I think with *"John Brown's body lies a-mouldering in the ground; His soul is marching on."*

Mr. Clarke then suggested that she write some good words for the "John Brown" air. She replied that she had wanted to, but so far had not found them.

That night in Willard's Hotel, Julia slept soundly until she awoke just before daybreak. And then the lines of the wished-for poem came to her. Determined not to forget them, she got up and in the dim light found a pen and some paper with the letterhead of the Sanitary Commission. Her own account follows:

> I scrawled the verses almost without looking at the paper. I had learned to do this when, on previous occasions, attacks of versification had visited me in the night, and I feared to have recourse to a light lest I wake the baby, who slept near me. I was always obliged to decipher my scrawl before another night should intervene, as it was only legible while the matter was fresh in my mind. At this time, having completed my writing, I returned to bed and fell asleep, saying to myself, "I like this better than most things I have written."

As an aside, we note here that the facsimile of the original shows that the handwriting is indeed difficult to decipher.

The familiar version of the "Battle Hymn" has five stanzas. Julia wrote six but later deleted the last. She gave the original draft to Mrs. Whipple, who had requested it. The final, revised version appeared in the *Atlantic Monthly* of February 1862, with an advance copy appearing in the January 14 *New York Daily Tribune*. Editor James Fields is credited with suggesting the title "Battle Hymn of the Republic." Julia received five dollars for her effort.

Publication in the *Atlantic Monthly* was a great honor, but Julia must have been disappointed with the remuneration. Earlier in the year she had submitted a poem to the National Hymn contest, the winner of which would receive $500. But no prize was awarded because the judges received nothing they considered worthy of the money.

Battle Hymn of the Republic

Mine eyes have seen the glory of the coming of the Lord;
He is trampling out the vintage where the grapes of wrath
are stored;
He hath loosed the fateful lightning of His terrible swift
sword;
His truth is marching on.

I have seen Him in the watch-fires of a hundred circling
camps;
They have builded Him an altar in the evening dews and
damps;
I can read His righteous sentence by the dim and flaring
lamps;
His day is marching on.

I have read a fiery gospel, writ in burnished rows of
steel:
"As ye deal with my contemners, so with you my grace shall
deal;
Let the Hero, born of woman, crush the serpent with his
heel,
Since God is marching on."

He has sounded forth the trumpet that shall never call
retreat;
He is sifting out the hearts of men before His judgment-seat:
Oh, be swift, my soul, to answer Him! be jubilant, my
feet!
Our God is marching on.

In the beauty of the lilies Christ was born across the sea,
With a glory in His bosom that transfigures you and me:

As He died to make men holy, let us die to make men free,
While God is marching on.

A twentieth-century scholar, Edward Snyder, has pointed out that Julia's familiarity with the Bible, her conviction of the justice of the Union cause and her ability to write verse all contributed to the success of her masterpiece. Some of the Biblical references cited by Snyder include Isaiah 6:5 and 63: 1–5; Psalms 18:14; Revelation 19:15 (And out of his mouth goeth a sharp sword, that with it he should smite the nations: and he shall rule them with a rod of iron: and he treadeth the winepress of the fierceness and wrath of Almighty God); and Jeremiah 25:15. Julia herself noted that a family acquaintance wrote verses; she particularly remembered two of his lines about revenge: *Wine gushes from the trampled grape, / Iron's branded into steel.*

Florence Howe Hall noted that her mother, a trained musician, wrote her poem expressly for what Mrs. Hall termed the "John Brown" air, and that the two cannot be divorced. However, the original copy of the "Battle Hymn" contained no hallelujah refrain, and the version sent to the *Atlantic Monthly* did not mention that the hymn was to be sung to the "John Brown" air.

Here are the first two stanzas of the "John Brown" song:

John Brown's body lies a-mouldering in the grave,
John Brown's body lies a-mouldering in the grave.
John Brown's body lies a-mouldering in the grave,
    His soul is marching on!

Refrain:

Glory, Hally, Hallelujah, etc.

He's gone to be a soldier in the army of the Lord,
He's gone to be a soldier in the army of the Lord,
He's gone to be a soldier in the army of the Lord.
    His soul is marching on!

Refrain:

Glory, Hally, Hallelujah, etc.

As the work became familiar, Northerners thought they were singing about the executed John Brown of Harper's Ferry fame. The original subject was, however, Sgt. John Brown who first enlisted in the 2nd Battalion,

Boston Light Infantry, Massachusetts Volunteer Militia and later in the 12th Massachusetts Infantry, both stationed at Fort Warren. He would drown while crossing the Rappahannock in June 1862.

Brown's comrades were amused that he had the same name as the fiery abolitionist, and they made up verses about the living subject. Vocal ensembles, including second tenor John Brown himself, sang them to the tune of a Methodist hymn popular at camp meetings and revivals. Here is its first stanza:

> Say, brothers, will you meet us?
> Say, brothers, will you meet us?
> Say, brothers, will you meet us?
>   On Canaan's happy shore.

Refrain:

> Glory, glory Hallelujah, etc.

In a short time trained musicians had arranged band music for the soldiers' improvisation. At a flag-raising ceremony on Sunday, May 12, 1861, the Brigade Band struck up the tune and the men sang the verses. Six days later the song made its debut in Boston, where recruits from Fort Warren sang it on the march. On July 23 the 12th Massachusetts Volunteers, commanded by a son of Daniel Webster, left for action. Frank Sanborn, who saw them leave, wrote this years later:

> I happened to be in Boston the day that Fletcher Webster's regiment (the 12th Mass. Volunteers) came up from Fort Warren, landed on Long Warf, and marched up State Street past the old State House, on their way to take the train for the Front, in the summer of 1861. As they came along, a quartette, of which Capt. Howard Jenkins, then a sergeant in this regiment, was a tenor voice, was singing something sonorous, which I had never heard. I asked my college friend Jacobsen, of Baltimore, who stood near me, "What are they singing?" He replied, "That boy on the sidewalk is selling copies." I approached him and bought a handbill which, without the music, contained the rude words of the John Brown song, which I then heard for the first time, but listened to a thousand times afterward during the progress of the emancipating Civil War....

(Sanborn was one of the members of the Secret Six.)

The next day, the 12th marched down Broadway to the strains of "John Brown." Four days later, the Hallelujah Regiment, as it would be called, was at Harper's Ferry and the "John Brown" song launched into a sea of popularity. Apparently there were ribald versions, and perhaps Julia's pastor was trying to bring about their demise when he suggested that she write some new words.

By this time C.S. Hall of Charlestown, Massachusetts, had put out a broadside with both words and music, noting Fort Warren as the origin of the tune. Even before Webster's regiment had left Boston, one Johnny Rounders, apparently intoxicated, was arrested for disturbing the public peace by singing "John Brown's bones dangling in the air," followed by hallelujahs.

The origin of the "John Brown" ("Say, Brothers, Will You Meet Us?") air is uncertain. Boyd Stutler, a John Brown buff, concluded after many years of study that it was "lost in the mists of years." He considered it a genuine folk-air, used as a Swedish drinking song or a sea chantey generations before either John Brown. He also suggested that it came to America via words written by Charles Wesley. James Fuld, author of *The Book of World Famous Music*, could find nothing to substantiate either idea.

Over the years there have been persistent claims that William Steffe (originally di Stefano) is the author of the air "Say, Brothers, Will You Meet Us?" Steffe contended that in 1855 or 1856 he composed the tune for a series of verses beginning "Say, bummers, will you meet us?" The composition was to be sung by the Good Will Engine Company of Philadelphia in honor of a visiting Baltimore fire company.

Stutler refutes this as well as the common statement that a Southerner wrote the music of the "Battle Hymn." He maintains that Steffe was born and died in Philadelphia.

When Charles Claghorn researched this, he contacted Edwin Steffe, grandson of William and a professional singer himself. In *Papers of the Hymn Society of America*, (1974), Claghorn quotes a letter from Edwin Steffe:

> William Steffe was the organist and choirmaster of the Indian Fields Camp Meeting Festivals that were held annually in Indian Fields, South Carolina. He wrote a marching hymn entitled "Say, Brothers, Will You Meet Us?" and some musical researchers have found this hymn to be the basis in form of the "Battle Hymn". . . . He also stated that William Steffe was a native South Carolinian, and referred to the Methodist Indian Fields camp meetings as "where the tune originated."

Claghorn notes that although Steffe was reported as being born in the South, he apparently moved to Philadelphia, since his name appears in the city directories there in 1856 and subsequent years.

Some authorities maintain that the tune is truly southern—like a plantation air—"very useful to pick cotton by," and suggest that it could have originated as a Negro spiritual.

To add to the confusion, or perhaps elucidation, there is a statement by Private James Beale, who was stationed at Fort Warren in 1861. He asserted that in the 1850s, a fire company in Charleston, South Carolina, commissioned a Philadelphia musician to write a chantey. Its opening lines were "Say, bummers will you meet us," but according to Beale the Methodists changed "bummers" to "brothers" and included the work in their Sunday School song books.

Fuld notes that the earliest known publication of the hymn tune appeared as "My Brother Will You Meet Me" in Charles Dunbar's *Union Harp and Revival Chorister*, published in Cincinnati in 1858.

Others besides Steffe have claimed authorship, and the matter may never be explained satisfactorily. It is clear, however, that this air of disputed authorship is a perfect setting for the "Battle Hymn." Despite enormous popularity during the Civil War, a combination of the "John Brown" words and the "Say, Brothers" tune, the "Battle Hymn" might have met the same fate as the rest of Julia's poems.

On January 1, 1863, when the Emancipation Proclamation became effective, Julia read her "Battle Hymn" to the huge throng gathered in Boston's Music Hall to celebrate.

The Baltimore Sun of February 4, 1864, described a crowded meeting held the previous evening at the Hall of the House of Representatives. The Christian Commission reported on its work with Union soldiers during the past year. Then "the Battle Hymn of the Republic was sung by Chaplain McCabe of Ohio, to the tune of 'John Brown's body lies moldering in the Grave,' which was repeated at the request of President Lincoln, the whole audience rising and joining in the chorus."

Early in the war a group of young women had offered to assist the Sanitary Commission. Chev's answer noted that "the men had enough of everything except noble watchwords and inspiring ideas such as are worth fighting and dying for." Apparently the crowd in the House that night considered the "Battle Hymn" a source of noble watchwords and inspiring ideas.

In May, 1863, the Howes suffered a great personal tragedy. Sammy, who was three and a half, died from diphtheria. That year, Julia began to keep a diary, and from it we know something of her devastation. Chev was no less disconsolate. Now 61, he suffered from rheumatism and heart disease; in addition, he was subject to recurring attacks of malaria and neuralgia.

Julia assuaged her grief by studying religion and philosophy. Very soon she was writing related essays. One on religion finished, she wrote in her diary, "I believe that I have in this built up a greater coherence between things natural and things divine. I therefore rejoice over my work and thank God, hoping it may be of service to others, as it certainly has to me."

With the prime purpose of helping others through her studies of philosophy and comparative religions, she began to plan a series of public lectures for remuneration. But she had reckoned without her husband's approval. A journal entry reads: "Last night Chev declared I must read my lectures without compensation. I think he is mistaken, but cannot disregard his wishes in this."

For a while Julia settled for reading in her home a series of six essays entitled *Practical Ethics*. Annie Fields, the wife of James T. Fields of the *Atlantic Monthly*, noted: "Mrs. H. provoked and sustained a philosophic-scientific conversation with the gentlemen which showed her knowledge of Compte, Spinoza, Kant, Hegel, and the like. She said that if shut up with 12 books, Spinoza would be one of them. Homer stood first."

When Dr. Clarke invited Julia to read her essay, *Duality of Character*, in the vestry room of his church, she accepted. Theodore Parker, who had died in 1860, had encouraged her to speak in public, so she was not going to be put off indefinitely. She could find satisfaction in the fact that the *Christian Examiner* published some of the essays. But it was becoming clear that speaking was her forte.

Within a few months she was reading her essay series to a Washington, D.C., audience "in obedience to a deep and strong impulse." When the Howes' old friend Sumner turned down her invitation to attend, she justified her position by writing him about her purpose: "My whole study has been to find that deeper vein of consideration which should show the reasons for the mistakes that men make, and the sins they commit."

Chev objected when Julia was invited to New York to read a poem at William Cullen Bryant's seventieth birthday celebration, but she accepted. The contention continued, and about a week after Lincoln's assassination, Flossy voiced criticism of her mother for crossing her father. But urged on by the Rev. Clarke, Julia gave another public lecture in Boston.

Julia was a very influential member of the New England Women's Club, founded to "organize the social force of women then working alone or in small circles." By 1871 she was president and was re-elected almost every year until 1910. She was active in forming women's clubs in various parts of the United States. It was the New England Women's Club that sent Julia as a delegate to her first meeting of the suffragists.

At the first feminist convention, held in Seneca Falls in New York in 1848, Elizabeth Cady Stanton's resolution on the ballot had passed with a narrow margin. It declared "that it is the duty of the women of this country to secure to themselves their sacred right of elective franchise." When the Civil War was over, the issue had come to the front with the 15th amendment soon to grant the vote to black men. Women such as Susan B. Anthony and Elizabeth Cady Stanton were incensed that their sex was not included.

These so-called radical feminists wanted a woman suffrage amendment to the Constitution, and formed the National Suffrage Association. The first constitutional amendment on woman suffrage was introduced in Congress by Senator S.C. Pomeroy of Kansas in December 1896.

In New England especially, where female antislavery societies had flourished, women had begun to realize their potentialities for organization and action. For instance, the New England Women's Auxiliary had collected and disbursed $315,000 in cash and $1,200,000 in supplies and stores to the war effort. But now many of these women felt that giving the male Negro the ballot was a priority; after that, they would fight for the right of all women to vote.

In 1868 Julia became president of the newly formed New England Suffrage Association, a group of more moderate feminists that included Lucy Stone, an Oberlin College graduate and former lecturer for William Lloyd Garrison's antislavery society. Prominent abolitionists who supported the group were Garrison himself, Thomas Wentworth Higginson of the Secret Six (and whom we shall meet later), Wendell Phillips of oratory fame and Rev. Clarke from Julia's own Unitarian church. This association was the forerunner of the American Woman Suffrage Association, a group that sought the vote through amendment to state constitutions rather than federal amendment.

There was much opposition to woman suffrage: brewery and liquor interests feared that women would vote for what later was known as prohibition; business interests assumed that female voters would press for labor and social welfare reforms; the South was not about to support the enfranchisement of Negro women or a federal amendment that would infringe on the rights of states to establish their own voting qualifications.

Although woman suffrage began as a white, northeastern, middle class cause, the two major groups spearheading it did not unite until 1890, when they formed the National American Women's Suffrage Association. In 1890 Wyoming entered the union with a state constitution that gave women the vote. Three years later Colorado voted for woman suffrage. Idaho and the new state of Utah followed in 1896. But progress was slow, and by 1913 only 13 states and territories were granting full franchise. However, World War I helped the cause by making it possible for women to demonstrate their importance to the work force. In 1920 the 19th amendment guaranteed to all women the right to vote. The long struggle had taken the time and effort of a large number of dedicated women and a smaller number of dedicated men.

The women's club movement and woman suffrage would demand much of Julia's time and ability over many years. These causes provided her with opportunity for travel and public speaking. Chev was in favor of allowing women to vote but he never became reconciled to his wife's lecturing. Their son-in-law, Henry Richards, observed: "It was a strange household with Grandmother Howe slipping off to lectures and conventions while Polish and Greek refugees flocked to Grandfather Howe hoping for employment, which he usually gave them." Richards wondered, "How could they pull together when her intellectual striving was so strong and he, always impetuous, was off and away on some inspired mission to help humanity?"

Although Julia often spoke on behalf of woman suffrage, her status in the movement did not approach that of Anthony, Stanton, Stone and others who came later, such as Carrie Chapman Catt. By the way, Miss Anthony sometimes introduced Julia as the author of *Battle Cry of Freedom*.

Maud, the youngest Howe child, remained at home until 1887, but by 1872 the other daughters were married and son Harry well-launched on his career as a geologist. The first grandchild also arrived that year. Chev's health began to decline severely in 1874, and during the last years of his life he was unusually difficult. A trip to Santo Domingo improved him slightly, and Julia enjoyed it too.

The Howes were no strangers to Santo Domingo. Chev had supported President Grant's scheme for the United States to annex the Dominican Republic. As a member of a commission to study the matter, he had been to the island in 1871. The next year, he visited Santo Domingo, the capital, with Julia, Maud and three of his nieces. Incidentally, Sumner, once Chev's alter ego, did not approve of United States interference in the affairs of this Caribbean country, and he was influential in blocking the move.

The last months of Howe's life seem to have brought true reconciliation between him and Julia. He died in January 1876. Florence Howe Hall states that many years after Chev's death, she suggested to Julia that the line *He has sounded forth the trumpet that shall never call retreat* should be used to honor her brother-in-law, about to retire from Perkins Institution. "No," said her mother, "that is for your father."

Howe's money was to be divided equally among his daughters, his wife having "ample means of her own." At the time of his death, his income amounted to a little more than $2000 a year. It took time and legal fees to straighten out ownership of the various properties. In any case, most of the land was a liability because of taxes. Julia was able to supplement her income by lecturing and writing, and during the 34 years of her widowhood she proved herself a good financial manager.

Even in her day, Julia believed that women should be ministers. In 1870 she delivered her first real sermon from a pulpit. Three years later she organized a convention of woman preachers. She was publicly opposed to a double standard of morality for men and women.

The Franco-Prussian War stimulated Julia to start a women's movement for international peace. Unfortunately, she was not successful in this effort.

As the years went by, Julia became a favored speaker, both for tours and on many diverse occasions. One especially noted lecture was her "Modern Society," given at the Concord School of Philosophy in 1879 to an estimated 1500 people. She retained her faculties, interests and sense of humor until her death in 1910 at the age of 91.

The attitude of Samuel Gridley Howe toward his wife seems, at least, repressive. But we must consider it within the context of his day, when it was socially unacceptable for women to speak before mixed audiences and to deliver sermons. Julia's preoccupation with learning was unusual but marks her as ahead of her time. Perhaps the repression she encountered made her such a firm advocate of women's rights. And she lived long enough to see the American woman possess the right to personal freedom, to education, to earn a living and to keep her wages, to own property, to make contracts, to bring suit, to obtain divorce for just cause and to keep her children as well as receive a fair share of a couple's accumulation during marriage.

Julia's feminist activities are well described in *Mine Eyes Have Seen the Glory,* a biography written by Deborah Pickman Clifford, a modern-day descendant. But important as those activities were, Julia is best remembered for the "Battle Hymn." And rightly so.

The work is still immensely popular. In their *Best Loved Songs and Hymns* James and Albert Morehead state: "Its thunderous eloquence is not exceeded anywhere in the realm of patriotic poetry, and may be equalled only by the 'Marseillaise.'" The "Battle Hymn" is heard repeatedly at events ranging from small concerts to huge state occasions; it was sung at Churchill's funeral as a tribute to his American ancestry. Its theme is similar to a thought expressed in Lincoln's second inaugural address, and the poetry approaches the grandeur of Lincoln's prose. Surely Julia Ward Howe, who prized literary achievement, would be pleased to know that *The Grapes of Wrath* and *Terrible Swift Sword* are the titles of books by distinguished modern authors.

In 1987 a 14-cent stamp was issued to honor the author of the "Battle Hymn."

Louisa May Alcott
Little Women

People confuse her with Jo March, the character she created, and forget that Louisa May Alcott had a life of her own. That life is known to biographers through family journals and extensive correspondence; some authors have analyzed Louisa's writings to conjure up her character traits, but information of this sort may be misleading. After she became famous, Miss Alcott revised her journal and deleted portions. She also burned some old letters, deeming them "not wise to keep for curious eyes to read and gossip-lovers to print by and by." But much factual material is available.

Louisa was born in Germantown, Pennsylvania, on November 29, 1832. She was the second child in her family, the first being Anna Bronson Alcott, born the previous year. Her father, Amos Bronson Alcott, was at the time in charge of a private school for small children. Bronson, as he was called, had been sponsored by a wealthy Quaker. But when this patron died, Alcott did not have the resources to keep a school going. So he took his family to Boston, where in 1834 he opened his Temple School in the Masonic Temple. Louisa's mother was Abigail May Alcott. Known as Abba, she was a member of one of Boston's leading families. She appears to have been given to mood swings, but on the whole was a strong woman.

Alcott was self-educated and his teaching methods unconventional but advanced. He read widely and considered himself a philosopher as well as educator. He was intensely interested in child psychology. From all accounts he was a good farmer and carpenter. Elizabeth Peabody, who afterwards introduced the kindergarten system to Boston, assisted him at the Temple School. Later she was replaced by her sister, Sophia, who would become Mrs. Nathaniel Hawthorne. Sophia was in turn replaced by Margaret Fuller, the feminist. The school soon became well known and was visited by such personages as Ralph Waldo Emerson and Harriet Martineau, the British reformer. The first praised Alcott, but the latter published devastating criticism.

Even Elizabeth Peabody became nervous about Alcott's liberalism. He discussed childbirth with his pupils and admitted a black child; his *Conversations on the Gospel* was considered irreligious by some Bostonians, many of whom were descendants of the Puritans. All this was too much for nineteenth-century Boston, and enrollment began to drop. By 1839 Temple School had failed, and Bronson was deeply in debt.

Louisa, known as Louie, did not attend Temple School. However, Bronson played an active part in his children's education, teaching them himself most of the time. There would be two more daughters: Elizabeth Sewell Alcott, born in 1835, and Abba May Alcott, who arrived in 1840.

Among Bronson's admirers was Ralph Waldo Emerson, who proposed that the Alcotts come to live in nearby Concord. The life in Emerson's transcendentalist community appealed to Bronson; he would do manual labor and have more opportunities as a philosopher. He rationalized that "a purpose like mine must yield bread for the hungry and clothes for the naked, and I wait not for the arithmetic of the matter." In 1840 the Alcotts moved into a cottage rented for $52 a year. From then on, Bronson had only sporadic income; there was a succession of homes; time and time again relatives and friends, especially Emerson, helped out; the proud Abba was forced to take in sewing. Obviously financial insecurity left its mark on the girls and would be the root of Louisa's near-compulsion to support her family.

Although Concord was a beautiful, rustic spot with its share of intellectuals, life for the Alcotts did not run smoothly. Bronson raised vegetables for the family, but they had little else to eat. At first he chopped wood for $1 a day for the few who wanted him. Then he decided that working for hire was morally wrong. He did give "conversations" in surrounding communities and for these he accepted charity. His topics included Man, Human Culture, Character and the like. Despite Bronson's lofty ideals, he appears to have been egotistical and sometimes almost tyrannical. It has even been suggested that though he appeared to let children think for themselves, he in reality controlled their thoughts. Elizabeth Peabody found him intolerant of the views of others, stating that he "only seems to look in books for what agrees with his own thoughts." At a later date, Rebecca Harding (soon to become Mrs. Clarke Davis) termed him the "vague, would-be prophet." Alcott even irritated fellow transcendentalist Theodore Parker, friend of Chev and Julia Howe. Although loved by his family, Bronson must have been difficult to live with. There is also some evidence that he was mentally unstable. Anna was his favorite daughter; perhaps Louisa soon sensed this. And his wife was too occupied with family and household cares to give Louisa the attention she craved.

At a very early age, Louisa was exposed to the abolitionist cause. Her maternal ancestor, Judge Samuel Sewell, had written one of the country's first antislavery tracts. Abba's brother, the Rev. Samuel May, was very active in the movement, as was her childhood friend, Lydia Marie Child, whose *Appeal in Favor of that Class of Americans Called Africans* was published in 1833. In 1847 Bronson housed a fugitive slave whom Concord's underground railway was able to get to Canada. Alcott considered the event "an impressive lesson to my children, bringing before them the wrongs of the black man, and his tale of woes." As an adult, Louisa declared she had never been able to decide whether she was made an abolitionist "by seeing the portrait of George Thompson hidden under a bed in our house during the Garrison riot, or going to comfort 'the poor man who had been good to the slaves,' or because I was saved from drowning in the Frog Pond some years later by a colored boy." She was three when an antiabolitionist mob prohibited the appearance of George Thompson, the British antislavery leader, at a rally. The mobsters then tied up William Lloyd Garrison and dragged him through the streets of Boston. To protect him, the mayor had him jailed. Whether Louisa remembered the incident or heard about it is open to speculation. At any rate, she became an unswerving abolitionist and later would extol John Brown's attempt to take the government arsenal at Harper's Ferry.

Although Harriet Martineau did not approve of Bronson's teaching methods, she took back to England a publication called *Record of a School,* Elizabeth Peabody's account of day-to-day events at Temple School. This fell into the hands of James Pierrepont Greaves, a businessman turned philosopher-educator. Greaves was impressed with Alcott's ideas and had begun to correspond with him. By 1838 Greaves and his followers had founded an experimental school in Surrey, naming it Alcott House in honor of Bronson.

During the winter of 1841–42 Bronson became deeply depressed, for nothing was going his way. When Emerson offered him $500 for a trip to England, Alcott was quick to accept. He sailed in May, leaving a younger brother to take care of the plowing and planting. When bill collectors appeared, Abba turned to the May family for help.

Greaves was dead when Alcott arrived in England, but the other promoters of Alcott House were impressed with the philosopher from New England. The upshot was that Bronson persuaded two of them to leave England and join him in establishing The Consociate Family—one of the experiments in communal living popular at the time. Bronson returned home in October, accompanied by Henry Wright, Charles Lane and the latter's young son William. The strangers moved into the Alcott cottage and through the winter made extensive plans for their New Eden. They also disrupted Abba's household; in no time Lane was teaching the girls, with Bronson banished to the kitchen. Before long, Wright took a mistress and had to leave the fold. Lane and Bronson found in Harvard a dilapidated house and barn surrounded by 90 acres. It was remote, but they thought it an ideal spot to gather together the followers they were sure to find. Lane

Louisa May Alcott. Courtesy Concord Free Public Library.

invested some of his own money and Sam May signed a note; Emerson did not involve himself in the scheme.

By June 1843, the Alcotts had moved to the newly-acquired Fruitlands. This was Abba's tenth home in 13 years of marriage. Louisa was ten at the time. Lane and Alcott had succeeded in interesting very few in the venture, so The Consociate Family numbered only 12. Living was Spartan. The group grew its own food and vegetarianism was practiced; everyone wore linen tunics (cotton involved slavery and wool deprived sheep of their covering); no leather was allowed because it came from animals; bathing water could not be warmed; cattle were not to be subjected to plowing; the brethren in this paradise would neither hire nor be hirelings; sexual abstinence in marriage, as practiced by the Shakers, was advocated — and so on. The impractical scheme failed in December, with Lane leaving to join the Shakers. For a time it had been touch and go whether Bronson would desert his family for the celibate life Lane advocated.

After Lane's departure Alcott went into prolonged deep depression. The whole Fruitlands episode was disturbing to Abba and her two older daughters. However, Louisa's biographers believe that Lane's culture and teaching had a beneficial effect on Louisa's literary career, although she disliked the man.

By 1845 Abba had used money left her by her father to buy a farmhouse that they named Hillside. Bronson worked very hard to improve the place and did succeed in making it comfortable and attractive. He planted a large garden and was rewarded by abundance. It was here that Louisa first had her own room when she was 13, and began to write poems, plays and short stories. She also composed romantic letters for Emerson, then 43, but never delivered them. A more mature Louisa would have real affection and admiration for the distinguished essayist.

Lizzie's (Elizabeth's) journal tells of berry picking, walks in the woods, picnics and the like when she lived at Hillside. And around this time, Louisa began to admire her father's friend, Henry Thoreau, some 15 years older than herself. Her new room had a door opening to the outside, so she could "run off to the woods when I like." From all accounts, she was a tomboy. She herself noted, "I was born with a boy's nature and always had more sympathy and interest in them than in girls."

When Anna was 14 and Louisa a year younger, they attended the district school in Concord—a departure from being taught by their father or Lane or female teachers. Louisa's education was hardly formal, but nevertheless she and her sisters were always encouraged to think and to read. She became familiar with a variety of authors, including Shakespeare, Scott and Dickens. The two older girls loved to act. They dramatized their favorite, *Pilgrim's Progress*, then turned to Dickens. By the time they were around 16, they had become highly skilled in writing, producing and acting their own very imaginative dramas. Both developed a lasting love of theater.

Abba and Louisa resembled one another in looks and temperament, and by now the bond between them was growing strong. "Mother understands and helps me," Louisa wrote. A few years later a journal entry stated:

> I often think what a hard life she has had since she married, — so full of wandering and all sorts of worry: so different from her early easy days, the youngest and most petted of her family. She is a very brave, good woman; and my dream is to have a lovely quiet house for her, with no debts or troubles to burden her.

On balance, Louisa and her sisters grew up in a loving atmosphere. Both parents instilled in their girls high principles. Louisa remembered some rules of guidance from Abba: *Rule yourself. Love your neighbors. Do the duty which lies nearest you.* Louisa noted:

> Our poor little house had much love and happiness in it, and was a shelter for lost girls, abused wives, friendless children, and weak or wicked men. Father and Mother had no money to give, but gave them time, sympathy, help; and if blessings would make them rich, they would be millionaires. This is practical Christianity.

Summers at Hillside always meant plenty to eat, but it was difficult to survive in the New England winter, especially when the family could no longer get credit. So when Boston philanthropists offered Abba a job at $30 a month "visiting the poor and investigating their wants and their merits," she took it. Hillside was rented and in 1848 the family went to Boston.

Their new home consisted of three rooms and a kitchen in the basement of a rented house. With Abba now a social worker and Anna a governess, Louisa, 16, would keep house. Lizzie, 13, and Abby May, 8, would attend school. Bronson had found a place where he was prepared to give his "conversations" if he could find interested audiences.

"The Missionary to the Poor," as Abba was called, had a relief room from which she dispensed clothing that she had collected. Boston was flooded with thousands of Irish immigrants who had fled the potato famine. Most were ignorant, unskilled and unused to city surroundings. They brought with them smallpox and a rising crime rate. To add to this, they were Roman Catholics, and that religion was shunned in New England. Abba herself once asked her employers, ". . . are we not building up Catholic faith on Protestant charity?" She preferred as clients German immigrants and Negroes. To her the latter were "far more interesting than the God-fearing Irish, who choke with benedictions and crush you with curses." When she found out black children were denied access to good schooling, she and Anna and Louisa taught them to read and write at evening classes.

Abba took her work seriously, reading philosophical works on organized charity and investigating the root causes of poverty. She blamed capitalism for most of the problems. "Employment is needed," she wrote, "but just compensation is more needed. Is it not inhuman to tax a man's strength to the uttermost by all sorts of competition that a certain result may be accomplished in a given time?"

The relief room proved so successful that gradually Abba became overwhelmed—for instance, in one December she had 210 cases. As the number of applicants increased, her volunteer sewing circle and other committees lost interest. Abba, in frustration, lashed out at everyone—employers as well as clients—and by the spring of 1850 she no longer had a position.

Urban life did not appeal to Louisa. She noted that "the bustle and dirt and change send all lovely images and restful feeling away," whereas, "among my hills and woods I had fine free times alone." By the time she was 15, Lizzie had left school to take over the family's housekeeping. This left Louisa free to teach, though she found it "very hard to be patient with the children sometimes."

During their stay in Boston, the Alcotts lived in many abodes. Abba's uncle offered them the use of a large house for the summer in 1850. This was most welcome since Abba had no work and Bronson was, to quote himself, "an unsaleable commodity." They had just moved in when Abba came down with smallpox, caught, according to Louisa, from "some poor immigrants whom mother took into our garden and fed one day." The contagion spread to everyone else in the family and Bronson almost died.

Before that summer was over, Abba started an "intelligence service," in reality an employment agency for cooks, nursemaids, dressmakers and the like. For the two years that she ran the business, she never earned more than a dollar a day and usually made much less. She was appalled by the exploitation of the women she placed as domestics, writing, "The whole system of Servitude in New England is almost as false as slavery in the South." Once Abba sent Louisa to one of her clients. Louisa felt mistreated and stayed for only seven weeks. She later described the experience in "How I Went Out to Service." Abba, who lacked endurance, soon gave up the employment service and took in boarders.

In 1852 Louisa's first story, "The Rival Painters, a Tale of Rome," sold to *Olive Branch* for $5. She had written it in Concord when she was 16. "Great rubbish!" she wrote in her diary. "Read it aloud to sisters, and when they praised it, not knowing the author, I proudly announced her name." That year Nathaniel Hawthorne purchased Hillside, providing enough money for the Alcotts to move to a decent home in a respectable part of Boston. Incidentally, Louisa had read with relish *The Scarlet Letter* when it was published two years earlier. Some of the literary works that appealed to her then were Carlyle's *French Revolution,* Goethe's poems, plays and novels, Plutarch's *Lives,* Milton's *Paradise Lost* and *Comus,* Schiller's plays, Mme. de Stael's works, *Jane Eyre, Uncle Tom's Cabin,* and Emerson's poems. When 1852 ended, Louisa had brought in $105 by teaching and sewing. But she was on her way to supporting herself through her writing.

When Louisa was 22, George Briggs brought out her *Flower Fables* in an edition of 1600. This was a collection of moral fables, originally written for Emerson's daughter Ellen. The enterprise brought her only $32, however.

Just before *Flower Fables,* "The Rival Prima Donnas" had come out in the *Saturday Evening Gazette* under the pseudonym Flora Fairfield. It was one of the "lurid" tales Louisa would write mainly for money, using a pen name. She later dramatized this story, hoping to get it produced. It is clear that she (and Anna) not only loved the theater, but at this point in their lives entertained hopes of becoming professional actresses. In the summer of 1855 in Walpole, New Hampshire, the two sisters founded an amateur dramatic society and performed plays "to an audience of a hundred and were noticed in the Boston papers."

Around this time Louisa wrote in her journal, "It's a queer way we live, but dramatic, and I rather like it; for we never know what is to come next. We are real 'Micawbers' and always 'ready for a spring.' "

With her parents and Lizzie and May in Walpole, Louisa returned to Boston alone to stay with cousins. She supported herself by sewing and writing. A few months later she returned to her family to help care for her younger sisters who had contracted scarlet fever.

The next time she went to Boston, she paid $3 a week for board and a room with a fire. During this period, Theodore Parker counseled her, as he did Julia Ward Howe. According to Louisa, "He is like a great fire where all can come and be warmed and comfortable. Bless Him!" And "Go to hear Parker, and he does me good. Asks me to come Sunday evenings to his home."

Boston was not only an intellectual center; it was a hub of the antislavery movement, and Louisa met, besides Parker, such people as Wendell Phillips, William Lloyd Garrison, Harriet Beecher Stowe and Charles Sumner. But perhaps best of all, Thomas Barry, the manager of the Boston Theater, gave her a pass to performances there. (She was also entertaining the hope that he would produce something she had written.) When Louisa left Boston in 1857 to summer in Walpole, she had written eight stories, taught for four months and earned $100; she had, of course, sent money home.

Later that year the Alcotts moved back again to Concord. It was now clear that Lizzie was dying of an emaciating disease, and Louisa became her competent chief nurse. Death came in March 1858, when Lizzie was not quite 23. Louisa, herself 25, wrote: "So the first break comes, and I know what Death means—a liberator for her, a teacher for us ... Death never seemed terrible to me, and now is beautiful; so I cannot fear it, but find it friendly and wonderful."

Another break came two years later when Anna, 29, married John Pratt, a Concord man who worked for an insurance firm. Louisa had a high regard for him but resented losing her sister. At the wedding, Abba, May and she wore gray dresses and roses. "Sackcloth, I called it, and ashes of roses," she wrote, "for I mourn the loss of my Nan, and am not comforted." Later when she visited the bride and groom, she noted that they looked like a pair of turtle doves, adding "but I'd rather be a free spinster and paddle my own canoe."

Louisa called 1860 the "Year of Good Luck" for the Alcotts. With Anna happily married, the remaining family were comfortably settled in Orchard House; May was coming into her own as an artist; after many unsuccessful speaking tours around the country, Bronson was employed as superintendent of schools in Concord; and the *Atlantic Monthly* published a story of Louisa's. "People seem to think it is a great thing to get into the *Atlantic*," she commented, "but I've not been pegging away all these years in vain, and may yet have books and publishers and a fortune of my own." And she had another bonus that year—a farce called *Nat Bachelor's Pleasure Trip* was produced. There was only one performance, but it was a first for her.

By April 1861, the Civil War had begun. Louisa joined other Concord women in making bandages and clothes for Union soldiers. When Dorothea Dix, a recognized leader in social reform, and now newly appointed Superintendent of Female Nurses for the Army, called for women to care for the wounded, she specified that "The applicant must be thirty, plain looking, dressed in brown or black." There were restrictions, such as "no bows, no curls, no jewelry and no hoop skirts." Miss Dix may have been trying to discourage camp followers and frivolous girls, but it was generally agreed that her rules were unrealistic and drove away many potentially helpful women. Louisa, now 30, because of patriotism, her bent for nursing and some desire for adventure, answered the call and in December 1862, was ordered to the Union Hotel Hospital in Georgetown, near Washington.

The capital city was overcrowded because of the war. Some so-called hospitals, such as Louisa's, were converted dwellings with totally inadequate facilities. Care of the sick and wounded was generally poor. Military hospitals often had more cases of typhoid, pneumonia, measles and other medical diseases than they had traumas. Surgery consisted mainly of amputations, and this all too often caused death from infection, since, of course aseptic techniques were not followed. Ether anesthesia was known, but Louisa noted that it was not considered necessary for amputations. The state of medical knowledge was so limited that little could be done other than trying to keep the patient clean and comfortable, feeding him when necessary and being with him when he died. Nurses, trained and otherwise, tried to make life more tolerable for the patients by writing letters, reading to them and comforting them, but there was little time for this sort of thing.

Louisa's first two days on duty were spent in a medical ward. On the third day, 40 horse-drawn ambulances brought in casualties from the Battle of Fredericksburg, where Lee's troops, at the Rappahannock, had wrought dreadful havoc on the Federal forces under General Burnside. Louisa was assigned to a ward for the seriously wounded—it had previously served as the hotel's ballroom. "Round the great stove was gathered the dreariest group I ever saw," she wrote, "ragged, gaunt and pale, mud to the knees, with bloody bandages untouched since put on days before; many being bundled up in blankets, coats being lost or useless; and all wearing that disheartened look which proclaimed defeat more plainly than any telegram of the Burnside blunder."

But her nursing career was short-lived. After serving for three weeks, Louisa became ill. When her condition became critical, Bronson hastened to Washington, hoping to escort his daughter home. The diagnosis was typhoid pneumonia, a condition almost unknown today. Louisa was delirious during the long train ride to Concord. For the next three weeks, Abba, Bronson and May took turns caring for their hallucinating patient. By March she was definitely improving, although her convalescence was slow. Apparently she was never again completely well, and modern biographers have blamed mercury poisoning as the cause of Louisa's continuing complaints. It is true that she received excessive doses of calomel during the illness, but it is difficult to appraise the extent of the damage.

Louisa was finally strong enough to organize accounts of her experiences at Union Hotel Hospital, and gave them to Frank Sanborn, who was then editing the abolitionist newspaper, *Commonwealth*. These "Hospital Sketches" were so popular that their author had offers to issue them in book form. Louisa chose as her publisher the rabid abolitionist James Redpath, who put out a 100-page edition for 50¢ a copy. Louisa never forgot her short stint of government service, for which she received $10. She said later, ". . . my greatest pride is in the fact that I lived to know the brave men and women who did so much for the cause, and that I had a very small share in the war which put an end to a great wrong."

Before her illness, *Frank Leslie's Illustrated Newspaper* had awarded Louisa a prize of $100 for her story "Pauline's Passion and Punishment." A "lurid" piece, she published it under the pseudonym A.M. Barnard. For the next five years, she would continue to write this type of thing, unknown to Bronson and his intellectual friends. If the works had no literary merit, the pay was good, and Louisa was a Yankee at heart.

In the summer of 1863 the *Atlantic* published "Thoreau's Flute," a poem that Louisa had written after the nature lover's death from tuberculosis. This is considered high quality, and of course Louisa must have been pleased to have it accepted by James T. Fields, the man who had advised her to stick to teaching because she couldn't write.

A very long adult novel named *Moods* had occupied Louisa for some time. Redpath wanted her to shorten it, but she refused. After she had revised it and cut out ten chapters, A.K. Loring published it in 1864. There were several poor reviews, which she blamed on the enforced cutting. She declared, "My next book shall have no *ideas* in it, only facts, and the people shall be as ordinary as possible, then critics will say it's all right."

According to Martha Saxon, a modern biographer of Miss Alcott, *Moods* is a flawed novel demonstrating remarkable insight, and based on Louisa's long-term secret infatuation with Thoreau. On the other hand, biographer Katharine Anthony suggests that the emotional situation of the novel was probably suggested by the crisis at Fruitlands involving Bronson, Charles Lane and Abba. Whether either one is correct cannot be known. After the success of *Little Women*, Loring reissued *Moods*, this time much to Louisa's dismay, though before *Little Women* was written, she had even arranged for its publication in England. In 1882 *Moods* came out again, drastically rewritten. Authorities have suggested that the first version of *Moods*, as well as Miss Alcott's anonymous and pseudonymous thrillers, represent the real Louisa better than her popular stories for young people. No matter what they represent, it is her books for young people that have endured.

In July 1865, she sailed for Europe as a companion to a sickly Miss Anna Wells, three years her junior. The crossing to Liverpool took nine days by steamship. After London and Brussels, the women made their way to Schwalbach where Anna was to "take the cure" at a spa. From there they went to a pension in Vevey, Switzerland. As time went on, Louisa found Anna demanding, and she yearned to travel independently. In November an ailing young Polish national named Ladislas Wisniewski was at the pension and soon became a great favorite. He appears to have been attracted to Anna. After spending the winter in Nice, Louisa was ready to go home in May; she had decided that her time was "too valuable to be spent in fussing over cushions and carrying shawls."

Paris was her first stop on the way back. There she met Wisniewski, the young man whose charm and musical talent had become familiar to her in Vevey. For two weeks he escorted her about the city, and she seemed to enjoy herself thoroughly. Some biographers believe that there was a romance between Louisa and Wisniewski, but in the light of the age difference between them, it does not seem likely. In addition, he had appeared to be more interested in Anna than Louisa.

Abba had borrowed money to enable her daughter to spend some time in England. Besides sightseeing, Louisa managed to sell the rights of *Moods* to a British publication for £5. By the time she returned to Boston in July 1866, Louisa had been able to store in her memory a wealth of new material for her pen.

About a year later she recorded, "Niles, partner of Roberts, asked me to write a girls' book. Said I'd try." Around this time, Louisa took on the editorship of *Merry's Museum*, but apparently did little about the book for girls. In September 1867, the request was repeated via Bronson, whose *Tablets* was in the process of being published by Roberts Brothers. This time Louisa took it seriously. For years she had thought of writing a story with the title *The Pathetic Family*, and here was her opportunity. She had already published stories that could be used as the bases of incidents. Even the family plays, written some 20 years before, could be incorporated into the story. Working at Orchard House, she finished the book in six weeks. On July 15 she recorded, "Have finished *Little Women*, and sent it off — 402 pages. May is designing some pictures for it. . . . Very tired, head full of pain from overwork and heart heavy about Marmee, who is growing feeble." Louisa was 35 when she produced her masterpiece.

Little Women was published in October and was immediately a great success. According to its author, it is "simple and true, for we really lived most of it." The story, now known as Part I, covers a year in the life of the March family during the Civil War. The girls are Meg, 16; Jo, 15; Beth, 13; and Amy, 12. The older girls work: Meg is a governess, and Jo reads to her rich and testy Aunt March. Their father is a chaplain in the Union Army; and their mother, Marmee, rules the household with a loving hand. There is little money to spare, and Marmee expects them to be selfless and endure poverty and tribulation without complaint. Next door live the wealthy Mr. Lawrence and his grandson Laurie. In time Laurie becomes well acquainted with the March family and particularly friendly with Jo, a tomboy type who yearns to be a writer. The girls love to put on theatricals, and Jo is especially adept at this. Laurie's tutor, John Brooke, falls in love with Meg, much to Jo's disgust. Marmee is needed in Washington when her husband becomes critically ill. To finance the trip, Jo sells her beautiful long chestnut hair, of which she is so proud, for $25. During the mother's absence, the gentle and lovable Beth contracts scarlet fever. Laurie wires Marmee to return, for Beth is seriously ill. But as Christmas approaches, all is well. Part I comes to a close as Beth begins to recover, Father March returns, and Meg becomes engaged to Brooke.

Louisa's diary entry of October 30 reads: "Saw Mr. N. of Roberts Brothers, and he gave me grand news of the book. An order from London for an edition came in. First edition gone and more called for. Expects to sell three or four thousand before the New Year.

"Mr. N. wants a second volume for spring. Pleasant notices and letters arrive, and much interest in my little women, who seem to find friends by their truth to life, as I hoped."

On November 1 she wrote, "Began the second part of *Little Women*. I can do a chapter a day, and in a month mean to be done. A little success is

The prototypes of Meg, Jo, Beth and Amy (clockwise from top left). Courtesy of the Louisa May Alcott Memorial Association.

Drawing for *Spider's Web* radio show—1983. Courtesy of Elliott Banfield.

so inspiring that I now find my "Marches" sober, nice people, and as I can launch into the future, my fancy has more play. Girls write to ask who the little women marry, as if that was the only end and aim of a woman's life. I *won't* marry Jo to Laurie to please any one."

The next month the Alcott home was closed up because Bronson was in the West and Abba was visiting Anna. May and Louisa went to Boston, where the manuscript of Part II was completed by New Year's Day 1869 (and without benefit of word processor or even a typewriter).

Part II opens three years after the finish of Part I. Meg becomes Mrs. Brooke, and soon she and John will have twins named Daisy and Demi. Jo is selling some of her stories, and May, now a beautiful young lady with artistic ability, goes to Europe as a companion to a March relative. She will continue art lessons while abroad. Jo takes a position in New York City as a governess. Here she becomes friendly with Professor Bhaer. When she returns home, Laurie proposes. She refuses him, saying they are too much alike. Then he too goes to Europe. While there, he spends much of his time with Amy, and after a while they decide to marry. Beth, the homebody, dies, cared for tenderly by Jo. Professor Bhaer visits the Alcotts. When he asks Jo to marry him, she accepts. Aunt March dies and wills Plumfield, her home, to Jo. She and her husband turn it into a successful school for boys. The book ends with a family reunion at Plumfield on Marmee's sixtieth birthday. The Bhaers now have two boys. The only shadow on the happiness of the "little women" is Amy's Beth, a frail child who may not survive. Mrs. March says to her daughters, "Oh, my girls, however long you may live, I never can wish you greater happiness than this!"

This skeleton merely summarizes the plot; it cannot convey the charm and warmth of the writing.

Louisa explains what is "true to life" in *Little Women* by listing events that really happened, though changed as to time and place: "the early plays and experiences; Meg's happy home." She added, "Mr. March did not go to the war, but Jo did. Mrs. March is all true, only not half good enough. Laurie is not an American boy, though every lad I ever knew claims his character. He was a Polish boy, met abroad in 1865. Mr. Lawrence is my grandfather, Colonel Joseph May. Aunt March is no one."

Louisa did not cut her hair, though she lost it temporarily during her severe illness. She did not marry, so Professor Bhaer was imagined. May's story did not correspond entirely with Amy's. At 37, the youngest March sister married a man from Switzerland. He was considerably younger than she, and not well off, but their short marriage seems to have been happy. She died in Paris a short time after the birth of a daughter, Louisa May Nieriker. It was May's wish that her sister Louisa raise the child, and little Louisa lived with her aunt until the latter's death.

Little Women is still in print. Millions have read it in English, and it has been translated into many other languages. The story has been dramatized for film and television. Best known of these productions is probably the 1933 film in which Katharine Hepburn played the part of Jo; a radio version was presented on the *Spider's Web* radio show in 1983 on PBS.

The success of *Little Women* enabled Louisa to pay off the family's debts. From then on, she was able to live comfortably herself and to provide well for the Alcotts. When Anna's husband died, she helped that family too, although they were not in bad straits.

Of course Roberts Brothers wanted more books like *Little Women*, and Louisa supplied the juvenile literature they desired, including *Old Fashioned Girl, Little Men, Eight Cousins, Rose in Bloom, Under the Lilacs* and *Jo's Boys*. She continued to contribute to magazines such as *The Youth's Companion, The Christian Register* and *St. Nicholas*. All this brought her wealth and fame. Ruth K. MacDonald in her 1980 book, *Louisa May Alcott*, states that "had [Alcott] not written *Little Women,* even with her adult books and her seven other juvenile books, her name would probably be an obscure footnote in the history of American writers."

Apparently Louisa was content to write in the vein of *Little Women* — homey, rather preachy stories that extolled virtues, but appealed to her readers. With regard to *Huckleberry Finn*, she wrote, "If Mr. Clemens cannot think of something better to tell our pure-minded lads and lassies, he had better stop writing for them."

If the characters in *Little Women* were not feminists, their creator was. Influenced as she was by Theodore Parker, Margaret Fuller and her Uncle Sam May, all ardent advocates of women's rights, it is not surprising that Louisa was intensely interested in the suffrage movement. In 1868 she joined the New England Woman's Suffrage Association; she signed the "Appeal to the Republican Women in Massachusetts," trying to secure votes for women from the state legislature; she was a frequent contributor to *Woman's Journal,* founded in 1876 by feminist Lucy Stone and her husband, Henry Blackwell; in 1876 she attended the Women's Congress in Syracuse; and she persuaded Niles in 1881 to publish *Massachusetts in the Woman Suffrage Movement* by Harriet Jane Hanson Robinson.

Perhaps partly because of her mother's influence, Louisa was interested in the economic as well as the political status of women. Marion Talbot, who knew Louisa, wrote this: "Inadvertently she once signed her name 'Louisa M. Alcott' instead of 'L.M. Alcott.' This time the check in payment was a greatly reduced amount. The publisher said his payment was always less for women. Many times later, when she was famous, he offered to pay her fabulous sums for her stories, but she told us of the delight she took in refusing to write again for his magazine."

By 1886 Louisa, who had never been robust since her wartime nursing experience, became seriously ill. Her mother had died in 1877. In 1882 her father had a stroke and was now becoming feeble. In 1888 Bronson died, and two days later, Louisa. They were buried in Concord, following a joint funeral.

Louisa May Alcott's books are less popular today than when they were written, but she is still remembered in the twentieth century. In 1940 a 5-cent stamp with her picture was issued. Helen Hooven Santymyer, author of the 1983 bestseller . . . *And Ladies of the Club,* has divulged that she was inspired to become an author by reading Alcott's works. That would interest Louisa, who maintained that the inspiration of necessity was all she had.

Henry James, at the age of 21, gave Louisa's *Moods* a negative review. But he noted, "There is no reason why Miss Alcott should not write a very good novel, provided she will be satisfied to describe that which she has seen. Miss Alcott doubtless knows men and women well enough to deal successfully with their every-day virtues and temptations, but not well enough to handle great dramatic passions. When such a novel comes, as we doubt not it eventually will, we shall be the first to welcome it."

In *Little Women* she described what she had seen, and thereby produced her enduring monument.

Emma Lazarus
"The New Colossus"

Today the name of Emma Lazarus is intertwined with that of the Statue of Liberty. The poem that is her enduring monument is familiar to most Americans, but few of them know much about its author.

Emma was no immigrant; her paternal and maternal forebears — both Jewish — were in this country at the time of the Revolution. She was born on July 22, 1849, the fourth of seven surviving children of Moses and Esther (Nathan) Lazarus. Moses was a wealthy sugar merchant who provided comfort and culture for his family. Like Julia Ward Howe's family, the Lazaruses spent their summers in Newport, Rhode Island. There was little anti–Semitism in New York in the mid-nineteenth century, and Emma recalled that she was brought up under American institutions, amid liberal influences.

Details about her schooling are lacking; she probably had private tutors. At any rate she was taught, besides the basic subjects, French, German and Italian. She also learned music and had a deep appreciation of it. Her sister Josephine described her as "a shy, pensive child, with strange reserves and reticences. . . ." From her earliest years, books were Emma's world, and in these books she literally lost and found herself.

In 1866 Moses Lazarus had his daughter's *Poems and Translations, Written between the Ages of Fourteen and Sixteen* privately printed. The following year Hurd and Houghton of Boston published the collection, which contained translations of Heine, Schiller, Dumas and Hugo. A second volume, *Admetus and Other Poems,* appeared in 1871.

Emma had met Ralph Waldo Emerson at the home of Sam Ward, Julia Ward Howe's literary brother. Emerson was then 64 and held in highest regard by intellectuals. To Emma he was "that font of wisdom and goodness." But this did not deter her from sending the celebrated man a copy of her first book. For some time he gave her constructive criticism, apparently seeing merit in her work. However, when he published *Parnassus,* an anthology of verse by more than 165 poets, nothing of Emma's was included. She wrote him that she could only consider the omission "a public retraction of all the flattering opinions & letters you have sent me, & I cannot in any degree reconcile it with your numerous expressions of extravagant admiration." Despite Emma's disappointment, her friendship with Emerson and his family continued. When he died in 1882, she wrote an appreciation of him for *Century*.

Emerson was not Emma's only preceptor. Thomas Wentworth Higginson, the writer whom we shall meet again soon, corresponded with her as a literary critic. Another mentor was Edmund Clarence Stedman, a well known poet and critic of his day.

By 1874 Emma had written *Alide*, her only novel. At 25, she was becoming a literary personage. As time went on, she published poems, translations, critical articles and reviews in such magazines as *Lippincott's*, *Critic*, *Century*, *The American Hebrew* and *Jewish Messenger*.

In 1877 Emma made translations from German texts of works by Jewish poets of medieval Spain. Later George Eliot's *Daniel Deronda* seemed to stimulate great interest in her Jewish heritage, and she began to write more about her people. There was also another powerful stimulus to come, as we shall see. But whatever the reason, she was, according to author Edward Wagenknect, one of the very first writers to strike an authentically Jewish note in American literature.

In a relatively short period Emma became a literary figure. In addition to her preceptors, she was admired by such people as John Greenleaf Whittier, William Cullen Bryant, Charles Dudley Warner, John Burroughs, and William and Henry James. She never married, and biographer H. E. Jacob suggests a strong emotional dependence on her father, accentuated by the death of her mother when Emma was 24. Ellen Emerson, Ralph's daughter, considered Emma "a pleasant—if somewhat intense—companion." Stedman described her as "thoroughly feminine and a mistress of the social art and charm."

Unlike American Jews at the time, Russian Jewry had been subjected to great repression. Following the assassination of Alexander II in 1881, Kiev and 150 small towns suffered pogroms. The fact that there were two Jews among the terrorists responsible for the czar's death provided an excuse to kill, injure and drive away Jews and to destroy or steal their property. Alexander III instituted laws that forbade them to live outside a town or city. This treatment was a spur to great masses of Jews to flee Russia. Those who reached New York stayed at the Immigration Station on Ward's Island. Here a temporary refuge had been set up with funds from Jacob Henry Schiff and the Hebrew Emigrant Society. Food had to be provided and problems of permanent residence in the country settled. The people were of all classes, but whether they had been rich or poor, all were refugees who brought with them little or nothing in the way of material goods. Emma's sister described them thus: "By hundreds and thousands they flocked upon our shores,—helpless, innocent victims of injustice and

Emma Lazarus. Courtesy of the Library of Congress.

oppression, panic-stricken in the midst of strange and utterly new surroundings."

Visiting Ward's Island with a rabbi, Emma was deeply disturbed by what she saw. The plight of such people became her great concern for the seven remaining years of her short life. In 1882 she described in a letter to *The American Hebrew* the quarters of 700 people.

> . . . the only appliances for washing consist of about a dozen tubs in the laundry and ten bath-tubs in the lavatory. Not a drop of running water is to be found in dormitories or refectories, or in any of the other buildings, except the kitchen. In all weathers, those who desire to wash their hands or to fetch a cup of water, have to walk over several hundred feet of irregular, dirty ground, strewn with rubbish and refuse, and filled, after a rainfall, with stagnant pools of muddy water in which throngs of idle children are allowed to dabble at will . . . .

She noted in the same magazine that ignorant and short-sighted philanthropy was far less helpful to the refugees than technical and industrial education. In response a nearby canning factory hired women and older children, and supplied boat transportation to get them to and from work.

In a span of two years 40,000 refugees arrived. Among them was Abraham Cahan, who later edited the *Jewish Daily Forward*. He noted in his autobiography: "When I arrived the immigration committee included one wealthy Jewish lady who belonged to the cream of the monied aristocracy. She was Emma Lazarus. She often visited the immigrants' camp on Ward's Island in the East River, but this never undermined her status as an aristocrat."

Putting her pen to work on behalf of her people, Emma produced between 1882 and 1884 22 essays and two editorials. In May 1882 she stated in a letter to the editor of *The American Hebrew:* "A few years ago I wrote a play founded on an incident of medieval persecution of the Jews in Germany, which I think would be highly desirable to publish now, in order to arouse sympathy and emphasize the cruelty of the injustice done to our unhappy people." She was referring to *The Dance of Death.* The magazine published it serially, and later, with other works, in a single volume entitled *Songs of a Semite.*

As more and more Jews arrived and competed with native-born Americans and immigrants who were already settled here, discrimination became a problem. ". . . [H]ere, too, the everlasting prejudice is cropping out in various shapes," she wrote. "Within recent years, Jews have been 'boycotted' at not a few places of public resort; in our schools and colleges, even in our scientific universities, Jewish scholars are frequently subjected to annoyance on account of their race. The word 'Jew' is in constant use, even among so-called refined Christians, as a term of opprobrium, and is employed as a verb, to denote the meanest tricks."

Familiarity with the immigrants made her a pioneer Zionist, declaring:

> [The Jews] have long enough practiced to no purpose the doctrine which Christendom has been content to preach, and which was inculcated by one of their own race—when the right cheek was smitten to turn also the left. They have proved themselves willing and able to assimilate with whatever people and to endure every climatic influence. But blind intolerance and ignorance are now forcibly driving them into that position which they have so long hesitated to assume. *They must establish an independent nationality.*

At the time the refugees were occupying so much of Emma's energy there was an ongoing drive to raise $250,000 for the pedestal of the Statue of Liberty. The statue itself had been proposed at a dinner party in 1865 by Edouard René Lefebve de Laboulaye, the liberal French jurist and scholar. He was discouraged because France was then under the repressive regime of Napoleon III. Laboulaye intended the structure to honor independence and be the effort of the United States and France, since both Americans and Frenchmen had died in the war that brought independence to the younger nation. Present at the gathering was a young and idealistic, but also able, sculptor named Frederic-Auguste Bartholdi. The conversation never left his memory.

With the building of the Suez Canal, he hoped to get a commission for a huge female figure whose lighted torch and headband might serve as a lighthouse. But his idea was not accepted. However, encouraged by Laboulaye, in 1871 he spent three and a half months in the United States promoting the idea of a statue that would embody principles dear to both countries. During the Franco-Prussian War, Prussia had received considerable support from this nation, which contained one and a half million German immigrants. Bartholdi's native Alsace was now part of Germany, and this gave him added incentive to stress the unique historic relationship between France and America. He discussed his project with such notables as President Grant, Charles Sumner, and Longfellow, showing them a sketch in watercolors of a huge statue in New York Harbor.

When he returned to Paris after a successful tour, Bartholdi was sure that he wanted Bedloe's Island, which commands the entrance to New York City, as the site for his Liberty Enlightening the World. He had an image of the statue on its pedestal rising from the ramparts of Fort Wood, a fortification on the island named for a hero of the War of 1812. The sculptor had envisioned a colossal Greek goddess holding a lighted torch in her right hand and broken chains at her feet. Ultimately under his direction there was constructed in France such a statue with an exterior of copper plates, a height of 151 feet and a weight of 225 tons; the left hand holds a tablet bearing the date of July 4, 1776; the face resembles that of the sculptor's mother. It is interesting that both France and the United States were receptive to the symbol of a woman, rather than a man, to represent liberty. (In contrast, a statue of Lafayette had been suggested.)

The original idea was to have the statue ready for the United States Centennial in 1876. But fund-raising lagged, and that was not possible. The French people eventually contributed $440,000, and by 1883, Bartholdi, working in Paris, had almost completed his work. Alexandre-Gustave Eiffel, the world-famous engineer, had designed an internal supporting mechanism. In 1885 the dismantled Liberty arrived, packed in numerous crates transported in a vessel provided by the French government.

The United States had agreed to provide a pedestal, but progress in this endeavor was very slow. With more than $100,000 collected, work on the foundation was begun. This was to be built at the site selected by Bartholdi and was under the supervision of Civil War General Charles P. Stone. After considerable difficulty and unexpected cost, a satisfactory concrete base was completed. The pedestal proper was designed by Richard Morris Hunt, an American architect trained in France, who produced a structure made of concrete faced with granite. But funds ran out before the pedestal was 15 feet high, and the work stopped.

The situation was embarrassing. Americans had been suspicious of France's gifts and not overly enthusiastic about contributing their share. But now an immigrant came to the rescue. He was Joseph Pulitzer, the Hungarian-born publisher of the New York *World*. He believed it would be "an irrevocable disgrace to New York City and the American Republic to have France send us this splendid gift without our having provided even so much as a landing place for it." He asked every reader to give something, however small, and promised to print the name of each donor. He also made the campaign attractive to working-class readers. Pulitzer was successful; in five months 120,000 contributions totaled $100,000, his goal, which was reached on August 11, 1885. Liberty's pedestal, 150 feet high and attached to a base consisting of an 11-pointed star — the ramparts of Fort Wood — was soon completed.

In 1883 Emma was asked to contribute a poem to a portfolio of original watercolors and literary contributions to be sold for the benefit of the pedestal fund. Emma at first claimed she could not compose to order. Then she had second thoughts. Remembering her experiences with the refugees at Ward's Island and drawing on the thought and imagery of her earlier work, she soon composed a sonnet that she named "The New Colossus." The statue was in Paris at the time, but she had seen pictures of it and knew the spot where it was to stand.

On December 3 William Evarts read the poem at the opening of an art exhibition whose proceeds were earmarked for the pedestal fund. Evarts was a prominent lawyer and had served as Secretary of State under President Hayes. As chairman of the Pedestal Fund, he had asked Emma to contribute a poem. Constance Cary Harrison intended to publish the portfolio, and she is credited with having persuaded Emma to write the famous sonnet. An art magazine reported that "$1500 was paid by Mr. Lydig Guydam for the portfolio of artists' sketches and of autographic contributions."

The New Colossus

Not like the brazen giant of Greek fame,
With conquering limbs astride from land to land,
Here at our sea-washed, sunset gates shall stand
A mighty woman with a torch, whose flame
Is the imprisoned lightning, and her name
Mother of Exiles. From her beacon-hand
Glows world-wide welcome; her mild eyes command
The air-bridged harbor that twin cities frame.

> "Keep, ancient lands, your storied pomp!" cries she
> With silent lips. "Give me your tired, your poor,
> Your huddled masses yearning to breathe free,
> The wretched refuse of your teeming shore.
> Send these, the homeless, tempest-tost to me,
> I lift my lamp beside the golden door!"

1883.

In 1813 Emma visited England and France. A second European trip in 1885 saw her again in France and England and also in Holland and Italy. Her British admirers included such personages as William Morris, Robert Browning and Thomas Huxley.

When the Statue of Liberty was unveiled on October 28, 1886, Emma was not present. A year later, at 38, she died of a malignant disease.

In 1903 an artist named Georgiana Schyler came upon the portfolio with Emma's poem. Through her efforts the words were inscribed on a bronze plaque that was affixed to an inside wall of the statue's pedestal. A copy of the poem in Emma's handwriting is now in the possession of the American Jewish Historical Society.

To understand the significance of "The New Colossus" to our heritage, we shall take a brief look at American immigration patterns and regulation in the nineteenth and twentieth centuries.

From its founding, the United States has been a nation of immigrants. The so-called first large wave of immigrants arrived between 1840 and 1860. About 16 percent were British, but most were Irish Catholics, forced from their homeland by a cruel potato famine. The majority of them began an urban life of poverty along the eastern seaboard; some joined canal- and railroad-building crews that took them west. Second in number to the Irish were the Germans, who with the Scandinavians were attracted by cheap land and farmlands in the Midwest. Many also put down their roots in Milwaukee, Chicago and Cincinnati. A good number of the Protestants were Lutherans, often led to the New World by their pastors.

The second large wave came after 1860 and reached its peak in 1907, when 1.3 million arrived. The bulk of these people were from southern and eastern Europe—Syrians, Russians, Greeks, Poles, Italians and Austro-Hungarians. There were also Japanese and Chinese. Of the Europeans, the Russians settled mainly in Nebraska, Kansas and the Dakotas. The others tended to work in textile mills and other industries in cities; many became miners. But relatively few were farmers, for land was now growing scarce. The most common motive for leaving their homes was poverty, and these second-wave immigrants were in general poorer, less educated and skilled than those who came in the first wave. Of the Asians, the Japanese were very successful farmers in the West, while Chinese laborers came largely to build railroads. Married women often had to remain in the homeland until their husbands saved enough for their fares to America. Chinese men seldom brought their wives for they intended to return to China. After 1880 it was common for single foreign women under 35 — typically Irish — to seek domestic work in New York and other cities.

Immigration was encouraged on both sides of the Atlantic. Abroad, a great increase in population had cut down the amount of land available for large farms, and the owners of small farms were finding it increasingly difficult to succeed financially. Many immigrants were seeking greater religious tolerance, while some were fleeing compulsory military service. The United States needed manpower to work its farms and mines and factories. As its society became industrial rather than agrarian, more and more workers of many types were needed. Letters from immigrants who had found work encouraged relatives and friends to come to the land of opportunity. An added incentive was the aggressive advertising by ship and railroad companies.

Between the 1840s and 1870s, steam began to supplant sail, cutting the transatlantic voyage to two to three weeks, with ships running on schedule. This is in contrast to the situation described in 1854 by a Dutch farmer. He noted that for four weeks, the winds had been "blowing out of the wrong quarter; hence no ships had entered the harbors of Holland, Belgium or Germany." This meant serious delay for innumerable people, who after already arduous journeys from their homes to ports, were forced to spend money for room and board while they waited for the departure of sailing ships.

Although the steamships were a decided improvement, there was still crowding and conditions in general encouraged the spread of the disease. Women were often at the mercy of male passengers and crew who chose to molest them.

During the 1850s self-provisioning by passengers was outlawed. Gone were the days when immigrants had to cook on the deck of a heaving ship. Seasickness was still caused by the heaving, but at least water and food, even if in short supply and of poor quality, were supplied.

Despite improving conditions in transportation, reaching America was a tremendous feat for many. Most of the emigrants were simple people who were subjected to exploitation at all turns. But still they came by the thousands, infected with "American fever." Of course there were adventurers and unscrupulous people, but in the main the newcomers were serious, hard working men and women with the courage to leave familiar surroundings in the hope and belief that they could improve their lot in an alien land. Castle Garden, New York, was the chief immigrant station from 1855 until 1892, when it was replaced by Ellis Island, which is close to Bedloe's Island. Between 1892 and 1954 Ellis Island processed 17 million immigrants. By 1987 their descendants number more than 100 million, almost half of the United States population.

As wave after wave of foreigners arrived, there was ultimately competition for land and jobs. Most of the new immigrants were willing to work for low wages, undermining the efforts of organized labor. With so many Irish in the country, there was great prejudice against Roman Catholics. The Japanese were loath to give up their Japanese citizenship, which made them unpopular. As we have seen, there was discrimination against Jews when their numbers became significant. With the arrival of Southern Europeans and Orientals there was concern that the Anglo-Saxon American stock was threatened. Incidentally, the term race was often used to denote ethnic background, and some people really believed that ethnic characteristics could be inherited. Businessmen feared that the foreign-born would spread ideas about socialism and anarchism. (We saw earlier that Emma Willard believed European immigrants would undermine the country's institutions.) This poem, composed in 1890 by writer Thomas Bailey Aldrich, expresses the deep animosity felt by some:

> Wide open and unguarded stand our gates,
> And through them passes a wild motley throng...
> Fleeing the Old World's poverty and scorn;
> These bringing with them unknown gods and rites,
> Those, tiger passions, here to stretch their claws.

Until late in the nineteenth century, legal entry to the United States was no problem. The immigrant's arrival date was recorded, and he was given a certificate to prove it. After a residence of five years, he could receive naturalization papers that entitled him to citizenship. Considering the situation and the inherent selfishness and bigotry that are part of human nature, restrictions were bound to come.

The Chinese Exclusion Act of 1882 was the first federal law to limit immigration of a specific ethnic group. Supported by Western laborers and racists, it was a violation of an 1886 treaty with China that guaranteed her people the right of immigration but not, however, of naturalization. With other acts that followed when it expired, the one in 1882 barred Chinese from entering the United States until 1943, when China became a World War II ally. Chinese already in the country were often subjected to harassment and discrimination.

A head tax of 50 cents was imposed on every person admitted to the country, and a law prohibited admission of anyone likely to become a public charge. But these measures had little effect on stemming immigration.

In 1885 the Foran Act outlawed the importation of contract labor. This meant that companies could no longer advance ship fare to the emigrant and collect it in small installments after the man began work. The Knights of Labor persuaded Congress to pass this after Hungarians and Italians had been brought in under contract to be used as strike-breakers.

By 1891 polygamists were excluded (we should note that the Mormons waged abroad a vigorous campaign to recruit converts to their religion), as were "persons suffering from a loathsome or dangerous contagious disease."

When Congress passed a law requiring all immigrants to take a literacy test, President McKinley vetoed the measure. But it passed in 1917, over President Wilson's veto.

On the West Coast, the Japanese were greatly resented because of their success in farming. The labor unions and Hearst papers led a campaign to prevent the entry of Japanese to the United States. President Theodore Roosevelt responded by working out a gentleman's agreement with the Japanese government that voluntarily restricted the number of their emigrant laborers. But that did not satisfy some factions; by 1920 Japanese were unable to buy or even lease land in California.

Further restriction of immigration was brought about by the National Origins Act of 1924 that based quotas on the ethnic backgrounds of the nation's white population. It was particularly restrictive against Eastern and Southern Europeans and excluded Africans and Asians except Filipinos. Immigration from nations of the New World was not yet regulated, but that would come.

The Displaced Persons acts of 1948 and 1950 allowed entry without regard to quotas of refugees from such countries as Hungary, Yugoslavia, Cuba and Indonesia.

President Kennedy wanted to see the end of national-origin quotas. He did not live to see that dream fulfilled. But President Lyndon Johnson, at the base of the Statue of Liberty, signed an act that abolished the system. The Immigration Act of 1965 permitted up to 120,000 annually from the Western Hemisphere and up to 170,000 from the Eastern Hemisphere. But no Old World nation was allowed to send more than 20,000 a year. Parents, spouses and unmarried children of American citizens were not bound by the limits. The act also gives preference to persons of exceptional ability whose services are sought in the United States. "The days of unlimited immigration are past," said Johnson. "But those who do come will come because of the land from which they sprung." Thus large-scale immigration from the Third World became possible.

With the Vietnam War and turmoil in Southeast Asia, Latin America, Afghanistan and Iran, the United States made additional provisions for refugees.

The 1980 national census counted just over 14 million foreign-born residents; 44 percent came from Asia and 29 percent from Latin America; Europeans made up less than 14 percent — a great change from the time when Miss Liberty was unveiled.

The problem of illegal aliens — especially from Mexico — continues to plague us. Some people believe that sanctuary should be given to illegal immigrants allegedly seeking political asylum; others do not condone breaking the law. While today there is less prejudice against Jews than there was a century ago, many Hispanics now feel discriminated against. The Immigration and Control Act of 1986 allows aliens who have lived and worked here since 1981 to apply for status as permanent residents.

It appears that immigration will pose problems as long as the United States remains a desirable place to live. In the past, immigrants helped this nation to become the envy of the world; whatever their origin, today's immigrants will help to shape its future.

Emma Lazarus' "New Colossus" is not considered her best effort by academicians who regret that her other works are no longer popular. But that one poem has given a special meaning to Miss Liberty. James Russell Lowell realized this when he wrote the following to Emma two weeks after the sonnet was first recited: "I must write again to say how much I like your sonnet about the Statue — much better than I like the Statue itself. But your sonnet gives its subject a raison d'etre which it wanted quite as much as it wants a pedestal. You have set it on a noble one, saying admirably just the right word to be said, an achievement more arduous than that of the sculptor."

At a later date, Louis Ademic did much to popularize Emma's poem. American children learn the last six lines, and no doubt the words mean more to those of European descent than they do to blacks, Hispanics, and Asians. But as children grow older, those lines can help them to understand America's heritage and do much to overcome their own prejudices.

The Statue of Liberty was declared a national monument in 1924. When Fort Wood was deactivated in 1937, the rest of Bedloe's Island was incorporated into the monument. Nineteen years later, it was renamed Liberty Island. Between 1943 and 1954, Ellis Island served as a detention center for aliens and deportees. It was made part of the Statue of Liberty National Monument in 1965 and opened to sightseers in 1976. In 1982 the Statue of Liberty–Ellis Island Centennial Commission of private citizens was created to raise funds for extensive restoration of the statue and the two islands.

Although the Statue of Liberty and Ellis Island are now part of history, future Americans today read Emma Lazarus' inspiring lines inscribed in marble at the entrance to the International Arrival Building at Kennedy Airport.

Helen Hunt Jackson
Ramona

The year was 1879. A group calling itself the Omaha Indian Committee was in Boston to make known the plight of the Poncas, a peaceful and agricultural Indian tribe. Chief Standing Bear, a Ponca in his sixties, spoke on their behalf, as did a young woman named Bright Eyes. There were others in the group, including Thomas Tibbles, a white man and an editor of the *Omaha Herald*. They claimed that the United States government had removed some Poncas from land that was legally theirs—land located in the northeastern part of Nebraska. The new land granted to them was in Indian territory, hundreds of miles to the south, and it had proved unsatisfactory for farming. Many Poncas, especially children, had died during the terrible trek south. Horses and cattle had perished also. When more than 150 of his people had died on the new location, Standing Bear with 30 other Indians journeyed on foot for three months to reach eastern Nebraska, where the Omahas had given them refuge. Then these Poncas were jailed for ten days.

But it was soon found that such arrest was illegal. A judge of the District Court of Nebraska declared them free, and they were released; but at the same time, they were prohibited from living on an Indian reservation. When they found an island in the Niobrara River, it was too late in the year to plant, and they were in danger of perishing.

Hoping to gain support for the Poncas, editor Tibbles, who had a record of involving himself in reforms, organized a lecture tour of the East. Money solicited would help the refugees and pay for suits to recover their lands. Standing Bear and Bright Eyes seem to have been the stars in the performance. Bright Eyes, otherwise Susette La Flesche, was the granddaughter of a French trader and daughter of an Omaha chief. She and her brother served as translators.

One who listened with great interest to the Committee's presentation was a middle-aged woman writer who happened to be visiting in Boston. Greatly moved, she submitted the story, as told, to the *Independent* in New York and to the *Hartford Courant*. The writer's name was Helen Hunt Jackson, and the Ponca eviction immediately spurred her crusade for justice to Indians. This crusade would occupy the few remaining years of her life and produce a lasting masterpiece — *Ramona,* a novel about California Indians.

Helen Hunt Jackson was born in Amherst, Massachusetts, in 1830, the daughter of Nathan and Deborah (Vinal) Fiske. The Fiskes were married by Edward Beecher, and there were close ties between the Fiske and Beecher families. A faculty member of Amherst College and a Congregational minister, her father was a Calvinist and much opposed to the more liberal thinking of Unitarians. Helen, whose middle name was Maria, was taught at home by her mother and attended private schools. Deborah, by the way, had attended Adams Academy under Zilpah Grant and Mary Lyon. It is also known that an aunt, perhaps to encourage a love of reading, gave Helen a gift subscription to the *Youth's Companion.* There were four Fiske children, but only Helen and her sister Ann grew to adulthood. At an early age Helen became an occasional playmate of Emily Dickinson, who lived nearby. Their friendship would be renewed later and continued by correspondence until Helen's death.

When Helen was 13, her mother died of tuberculosis. Helen was soon sent to Falmouth, Massachusetts, to live with an aunt. Here she enrolled at Falmouth Female Seminary. Later she entered the famous Ipswich Female Seminary, mentioned earlier. Incidentally, she rebelled against going to Mount Holyoke "to learn to make hasty pudding and clean gridirons."

Three years after his wife's death, Nathan Fiske died in Jerusalem of dysentery. He had gone there in search of a cure for tuberculosis. Helen's maternal grandfather provided for her and Ann, and the year 1849 saw her living in New York City at the home of her father's clergyman friend, John Abbot. She loved New York, with all its advantages, and was fortunate in being able to attend Springler Institute, owned and run by John Abbott's brother. Helen enjoyed Springler and was considered a good scholar.

In 1851 Helen was visiting in Albany, New York, at the home of a clergyman friend of her father's. Here she met Lieutenant Edward Bissell Hunt, an engineer with the coast survey, whom she married the following year. The Hunts' first son was born in 1853 but died before his first birthday. A second son, Warren Horsford, but known as Rennie, was born in 1855. In 1860 the Hunts attended the Amherst College commencement, and at this time called on Emily Dickinson. During the Civil War, Hunt, now a major, had a fatal accident while working on an experimental submarine.

During Helen's life with Hunt, the issue of slavery had become important. The couple had lived in various parts of William Lloyd Garrison's New England, so she must have been aware of the growing conflict. But she took no part in it. She also failed to take a stand on women's rights. It is known that Edward Hunt disliked any kind of controversy, so perhaps this accounts for his wife's apparent lack of interest in two of the day's most significant issues. Hunt was not a churchgoer though he read the Bible every day. Helen herself showed very little interest in religion, making her worlds apart from Emma Willard, Mary Lyon, Harriet Beecher Stowe, Julia Ward Howe and of course her own father.

Within two years of Edward's death, Helen lost Rennie. He was only nine and, like the Howes' Sammy, succumbed to diphtheria. His loss devastated her, but she burdened no one with her grief. As she recovered she turned to writing. Encouraged by the editor, she submitted some verses to the *New York Evening Post. The Nation* also accepted a poem. Both were published under the pseudonym Marah. Her first prose submission was a description of Bethlehem, New Hampshire, where she sometimes went to try to avoid hay fever. The article appeared in the *Post,* and this time she used the initials HH, which would soon become well known to the reading public. In times she would use other pseudonyms — Rip Van Winkle, Saxe Holme — and would even write "No Name" novels. Often she left editorials and book reviews unsigned.

Newport, Rhode Island, was familiar to Helen because her husband had once been stationed there during their marriage. In 1866 she returned to this seaside town, renting rooms at a Mrs. Dames' literary boarding house, where she would remain for five winters. She had by now some success in publication and was determined to establish herself as a professional writer. At Mrs. Dames' she met Thomas Wentworth Higginson who was to be her literary mentor for the rest of her life.

Higginson, then 42, was well known. A Unitarian minister whose views were too liberal even for some Unitarians, he had been a passionate abolitionist, opposed to the fugitive slave law and supportive of John Brown's action at Harper's Ferry. During the Civil War he had commanded the First Carolina Volunteers, one of the early Negro regiments in the Union Army. He was an advocate of women's rights, temperance and fair labor practices. After the war, Higginson pursued a literary career and was a recognized contributor to the *Atlantic Monthly.* He seemed willing to give Helen advice, and she was prepared to take it.

The critics had a good word for her. As early as 1868, Higginson called her "one of the most gifted poetesses in America." Even Emerson admired her poetry. In 1874 he included five of her poems in an anthology entitled *Parnassus,* and in its preface stated, "The poems of a lady who contents herself with the initials H.H. in her book published in Boston (1874) have rare merit of thought and expression and will reward the reader for the careful attention which they require." But despite praise from Higginson and Emerson, Helen's poetry is no longer read. Higginson himself is now best remembered in connection with another poet; he was an editor of some of Emily Dickinson's poems.

March

Beneath the sheltering walls the thin snow clings, —
Dead winter's skeleton, left bleaching, white,
Disjointed, crumbling, on unfriendly fields.
The inky pools surrender tardily
At noon, to patient herds, a frosty drink
From jagged rims of ice; a subtle red
Of life is kindling every twig and stalk
Of lovely meadow growths; the willows wrap
Their stems in furry white; the pines grow gray
A little in the biting wind; mid-day
Brings tiny burrowed creatures, peeping out
Alert for sun.
   Ah March! we know thou art
Kind-hearted, spite of ugly looks and threats,
And, out of sight, art nursing April's violets!

From *Poems* by Helen Hunt Jackson, Arno Press, 1972.
Originally published by Roberts Brothers, 1892.

In 1871 Helen began to write short stories under the name Saxe Holme, usually for *Scribner's Monthly*. According to Higginson, by 1874 she was a very prosperous author; she seems to have been an astute businesswoman and quite aggressive about demanding high pay for her work. So in a relatively short time Helen became prominent in the literary circles of her day. And she credited much of her success to the man who had helped her in the beginning and who would continue to help her. She wrote to Charles Dudley Warner, editor and author, "Col. Higginson, as perhaps you know, is my mentor—my teacher—the one man to whom and to whose style, I chiefly owe what little I have done in literature. . . ."

One of Higginson's biographers, Mary Anna Wells, suggests that Higginson may have been in love with Helen. Wells makes it clear that she has no proof of this, and speculates that if it had been so, Higginson was not the type of man to leave his invalid wife. Fourteen years after Helen's death, Higginson described her as "the most brilliant, impetuous and thoroughly individual woman of her time." At the same time, we should note that according to Higginson's first wife, he often used superlatives. Referring to when he first knew Helen, he wrote, "She loved society, was personally very attractive, dressed charmingly, and had many friends of both sexes."

Helen's fame brought her into contact with many well-known persons. These included Charlotte Cushman, the actress; Anna Leonowens of

Siamese Court fame; Julia Ward Howe and Louisa May Alcott, both of whom we have met previously. Later she would meet Harriet Beecher Stowe who was still producing novels, and Mark Twain. Higginson once escorted Helen to Boston to hear Dickens read.

With travel writing lucrative, Helen was able to leave Newport in summer, staying in New Hampshire usually and visiting such places as Vermont and Nova Scotia. She even managed to spend 1869 touring Europe. When she made her first trip to California, she recounted her experiences in letters to the *Independent*. Because of ill health, she spent the summer of 1874 in Colorado Springs. Here she met William Sharpless Jackson, the man who would become her second husband.

Jackson, a Quaker, was a prosperous businessman, actively associated with both railroads and banking. His ventures took him to various parts of the country, sometimes for long periods of time, but Colorado Springs was his base. The marriage took place in 1875 when he was 39 and she was 45. Helen's new home was a charming house with a magnificent view of the mountains. Always noted for her good taste and love of beauty, she furnished it with pictures and pieces she had found in Europe. Colorado Springs was five miles from the foot of Pike's Peak. Only a few years old, it was growing rapidly and already had a population of around 3000. But mining, ranching and homesteading families were quite different from Helen's intellectual and literary associates, and she seems to have missed New England. Obviously, she no longer needed writing to support her, but during the years of her marriage to Jackson, she continued to turn out a large volume of literature, including pieces for children. Apparently her husband did not object to extensive travel connected with it.

During 1876 Helen wrote the novel *Mary Philbrick's Choice*. It was published by Roberts Brothers of Boston as part of the "No Name" series. Her editor was Thomas Niles, the man who had urged Louisa May Alcott to write a book for girls. Apparently Helen thought that Emily Dickinson might agree to submit a poem to a poetry anthology in the same series. A letter to Emily shows that Helen was aware of her friend's reluctance to publish. She wrote, "You are a great poet — and it is wrong to the day you live in, that you will not sing aloud. When you are what men call dead, you will be sorry you were so stingy." In 1878 Helen broached the subject in another letter:

> Would it be of any use to ask you once more for one or two of your poems, to come out in the volume of "no name" poetry which is to be published before long by Roberts Bros.? If you will give me permission I will copy them — sending them in my own handwriting — and promise never to tell any one, not even the publishers, whose the poems are. Could you not bear this much publicity? Only you and I would recognize the poems.

I wish very much you would do this—and I think you would have much amusement in seeing to whom the critics ... would ascribe your verses.

A few months later when Helen and Will visited Emily in Amherst, Helen tried again. The next day she said in a letter to Emily, "Now will you send me the poem? No—will you let me send the 'Success'—which I know by heart—to Roberts Bros. for the Masque of Poets? If you will, it will give me great pleasure." This time Helen got her way. On December 8, 1878, she wrote from Colorado Springs, "I suppose by this time you have seen the Masque of Poets. I hope you have not regretted giving me that choice bit of verse for it."

The literary event that brought Helen to Boston in 1879 was the celebration of Oliver Wendell Holmes' seventieth birthday. He was born on August 29, but the *Atlantic* saw fit to host the party on December 3. (They observed Harriet Beecher Stowe's seventieth birthday on the day she became 71.) Women authors had not been invited to Whittier's seventieth, two years before, but some, including Harriet, Louisa and Helen herself, had sent regrets, and intimated that the *Atlantic* was about to have competition in the form of an all-women magazine. The powers that be at that illustrious magazine were not sure whether these ladies were serious or joking; at any rate, females were in evidence at the Holmes affair. Helen sat at the head table between Whittier, who did not care for her, and Charles Dudley Warner, her friend, who read a poem she had written in honor of Holmes.

Just before this event, Helen had heard Standing Bear's story. Up to the Civil War, most Americans had been more sympathetic to the plight of the Negro than to the plight of the native American. Although Helen had shown little interest in abolitionism, she was now ready to fight with zeal for the right of the Indian.

With westward migration, Indian fields and hunting grounds were ruthlessly usurped by the white man. Treaties usually favored the government; the Indians were often deceived about the transactions they agreed to; in addition the new settlers little understood the people they had evicted, considering them inferior barbarians.

By 1806 the Shawnee chief, Tecumseh, had organized all the tribes east of the Mississippi into a confederacy to resist onslaught. But in 1811 General William Henry Harrison crushed Tecumseh's confederacy at their camp on Tippecanoe Creek near the Wabash River in Indiana. During his administration, Andrew Jackson aggressively encouraged enforced migration, and large migrations took place between 1820 and 1840. The Indian Removal Act of 1830 authorized the president to exchange western prairie land not wanted by whites for valuable land within state borders. The Indians had to vacate the traded land. Some Northern tribes did not resist, but members of the Five Civilized Tribes from the Southeast— Chickasaw, Choctaw, Seminole, Cherokee and Creek—fought removal.

Under military coercion, the trek to Indian teritory in what is now Oklahoma caused great suffering. Of some 11,500 Cherokees forced westward in the winter of 1838–39, about 4000 died along the way from disease and exposure. This journey came to be known as "the Trail of Tears." Osceola, the Seminole chief, induced his people and some runaway slaves to hold out for seven years in the Florida Everglades. The operation was costly to the Army, but in the end most of the Seminoles perished and Osceola was captured by treachery.

When Chief Black Hawk in 1832 led a band of about 1000 Sac and Fox men, women and children into Illinois in search of fertile land for his starving people, he was attacked by militia and regular Army troops. Fewer than 150 of his band survived. The experience of Black Hawk was typical; tribes found that the new land was frequently less fertile than the old. Henry Clay, the senator from Kentucky, denounced the state of Georgia for its treatment of the Cherokees, but most Americans showed what Ralph Emerson termed "deafness to screams of mercy with regard to forced removal."

The government had guaranteed that the land west of a line extending from the Wisconsin territory to the western borders of Missouri and Arkansas belonged "forever" to the Indians. But this was not to be. The settlers' greed for land and gold was insatiable; after signing agreements they misunderstood, the Indians refused to be confined to definite areas; corruption among government agents was prevalent; railroads were built; thousands of buffalo were slaughtered by whites—all of these were factors that contributed to continuing conflict between the two races. When gold was discovered in Colorado in 1858, the government brought from the Indians a great deal of territory in that state, displacing the Cheyenne and Arapahos to poor land in southeastern Colorado. Even here they were not safe. In 1864 about 500 Cheyenne, of whom roughly 100 were braves, were attacked by a force of some 700 that were either United States soldiers or First Colorado Cavalrymen. More than 100 of the Indians died. An officer present called it "murder, in every sense of the word," explaining that when he had remonstrated with the commanding colonel, he was told, "Damn any man who sympathizes with the Indians." Here is testimony from another officer. The action took place three days after the battle.

There was one little child, probably three years old, just big enough to walk through the sand. The Indians had gone ahead, and this little child was behind, following after them. The little fellow was perfectly naked, travelling in the sand. I saw one man get off his horse at a distance of about 75 yards and draw up his rifle and fire. He missed the child. Another man came up and said, "Let me try the son of a b----. I can hit him." He got down off his horse, kneeled down, and fired at the little child, but he missed him. A third man came up, and made a similar remark, and fired, and the little fellow dropped.

The miners applauded the colonel for bringing peace to the area. Although his action did elicit protests from some, including the Commissioner of Indian Affairs, no one was ever punished.

Two years later, Chief Red Cloud led more than 2000 Sioux against an Army force of 81 and was victorious. This was retaliation for building a road that invaded Sioux hunting grounds. It was made to accommodate the gold miners, this time in the Montana Territory.

The Sioux struck again in 1876 at the Little Big Horn River in Montana. Led by Chief Crazy Horse, they killed Colonel George Custer and his 264 cavalrymen.

The next year the Army routed Chief Joseph's Nez Perce Indians as they fled to Canada.

Her enthusiasm kindled by the Ponca delegation, Helen put all her energy into working on behalf of the Indians. Sometimes she used the public press; sometimes she depended on private letters to ministers, Army officials, college presidents, legislators and the like. To her credit, she used government records, housed in the Astor Library in New York City to back up her assertions. Via published letters, she had exchanges with Carl Schurz who was then serving as secretary of the interior, and also with William N. Byers, former editor of the *Rocky Mountain News.* The letters to Schurz involved the Poncas while the correspondence with Byers concerned the refusal of the Department of the Interior to issue rations to 4000 Utes in Colorado when only 400 were involved in action against the government. Helen made it clear in both cases that defense of governmental action was weak indeed. Between January and May of 1880, she assembled facts into a book entitled *A Century of Dishonor/A Sketch of the United States Government's Dealing with Some of the Indian Tribes.* She noted that "All of the quotations in this book, where the name of the authority is not cited, are from Official Reports of the War Department or the Department of the Interior." Some excerpts show the nature of this work.

The Delawares
This little handful—81 in number—is all that now remains to bear the name of that strong and friendly people to whom, little more than 100

years ago, we promised that they should be our brothers forever, and be entitled to a representation in our Congress.

* * *

The Cheyennes
They were pursued and slain for venturing to leave this very reservation, which, it appears, is not their reservation at all, and they have no legal right to it. Are there any words to fitly characterize such treatment as this from a great, powerful, rich nation, to a handful of helpless people?

* * *

The Sioux
Quotation from Report of the Indian Bureau—1879:
It is no longer a question whether Indians will work. They are steadily asking for opportunities to do so, and the Indians who today are willing and anxious to engage in civilized labor are largely in the majority; . . . There is almost universal call for lands in severalty; . . . there is a growing desire to live in houses; the demand for agriculture implements and appliances, and for wagons and harness for farming and freighting purposes, is constantly increasing.

* * *

The Cherokees
Quotation from Report of the Indian Bureau—1870s:
They are an intelligent, temperate, and industrious people, who live by the honest fruits of their labor, and seem ambitious to advance both as to the developement of their lands and the convenience of their homes. In their council may be found men of learning and ability; and it is doubtful if their rapid progress from a state of wild barbarism to that of civilization and enlightenment has any parallel in the history of the world. What required 500 years for the Britons to accomplish in this direction they have accomplished in 100 years.

In the Introduction, Helen wrote that the hope of righting past wrongs "lies in the appeal to the heart and conscience of the American people." The *Century of Dishonor* finished, its author sailed for Europe and gave Higginson the job of proofreading her manuscript. It was published by Harper and Brothers in January 1881. Helen hoped that Congress, once informed, would "cut short our nation's record of cruelties and prejudices." With this in mind, she sent at her own expense a copy to each member.

By March Congress had ruled that the Poncas be reimbursed for their losses; in addition, members of that tribe were to be granted some choice in land and given funds for houses, schools and teachers. This was some progress, which obviously she had helped bring about.

Helen returned to Colorado in May 1881, having spent the winter in the East. During this time, Joseph, B. Gilder, publisher of the *Critic,* was editing a novel called *Ploughed Under; The Story of an Indian Chief: Told by Himself,* by William Justin Harsh. Harsh's father was a minister and member of the Omaha Ponca Committee, and Bright Eyes wrote the Introduction. It appeared that the book would not help the Indians in the same way that *Uncle Tom's Cabin* had helped the Negroes. When Gilder suggested that Helen should write a novel, she was interested, but said that she lacked the requisite background. Soon afterward, *Harper's Magazine* wanted her to do a series of sketches on California life, but Will Jackson's business affairs were such that he could not go along, as originally planned, and she had to decline the offer.

Helen was eager to visit California again, realizing that there would be opportunity to study the Mission Indians of that state. She now persuaded *Century Magazine* to commission a series of articles, and the winter of 1881–82 found her in Los Angeles, the city that had just installed a telephone exchange and boasted electric light and one good cement sidewalk.

California's history differs markedly from that of states on the eastern seaboard. A Spanish possession from mid-eighteenth century, Father Junipero Serra established there a Franciscan mission in San Diego in 1769. Later, 20 additional missions were founded, stretching along the coast to Sonoma. The padres tried to Christianize the Indians. They taught them farming and crafts and used them to irrigate and perform other labors. The missions traded hides, tallow, wine, brandy, olive oil, grain and leatherwork for manufactured goods from New England, all transported around Cape Horn in Yankee ships. In time the missions became large agricultural enterprises; as small garrisons they also maintained Spanish control over the area.

After Mexico became independent of Spain in 1821, there was a move to distribute the productive land controlled by the church. The Secularization Edict of 1834 finally broke the power of the missions and forced out the church. When the Mexican government parcelled out the Franciscan missions to political favorites, thousands of Indians took to the woods to live in primitive conditions. Thousands were cruelly exploited by the new masters, and the population declined. By 1841 the first wagon train had left Missouri bound for California. Seven years later, Mexico signed the Treaty of Guadalupe Hidalgo, ceding to the United States an area that included California. Now the Mission Indians had little chance to assert themselves.

Before reaching California, Helen had of course obtained letters of introduction to persons able to help her. Through the Roman Catholic Bishop of Monterey and Los Angeles, she was fortunate in becoming acquainted

Helen Hunt Jackson. Courtesy Library of Congress.

with Don Antonio Coronel, who gave her much information about the city under both the Spanish and the Mexicans. He had once been Inspector of Southern Missions and was sympathetic to the Indians; he had a good knowledge of the laws governing them. He and his wife, Marianna, advised Helen about where to find old ranches and missions. It was they who suggested that she visit the del Valle ranch at Camulos because it still represented the life of a California rancho. As it turned out, the owner was away when Helen went there; nevertheless, it is widely held that she had in mind the del Valle ranch home when she later described in *Ramona* the Moreno house.

Within six months, Helen had visited all the missions from San Diego to San Francisco; she had seen ranches, Indian villages, canyons and other remote places. The story of Indians being removed from land granted to them became all too familiar to her. *Century Magazine* supplied her with a young artist who made appropriate illustrations to accompany her writing. Helen's observations and experiences during this period would be used later in *Ramona*, but her immediate concern was to obtain material for the commissioned articles. She researched records, used libraries and interviewed people. One of these was Father A.D. Ubach of San Diego, with whom she drove many miles to see places of interest to her. A dedicated friend of the Indians, he would be represented in *Ramona* as Father Gaspara, the priest who married the lead characters. California's first Indian school was located in Saboba. Mary Sheriff, the teacher, then had 40 pupils. She described Helen as follows:

> She was fair and blue-eyed with blonde hair turning gray, which she wore curled around a smooth brow. She was plump, but of neat form, weighing about 150 pounds, and was about five feet, three inches in height ... When she came to San Jacinto she wore a gray travelling dress, with gray bonnet to match, upon which was the head of a very large gray owl.

As Helen visited in the village, she asked the teacher if it would be possible to go inside one of the adobe houses. According to Miss Sheriff:

> A young and rather pretty Indian woman invited us to enter. Her baby was ill and she had it in just such a cradle, made of twigs woven together, as Mrs. Jackson afterwards described in Ramona. The mother said she feared the baby would die. Then with quivering lips she said: "We sent to San Bernardino for a doctor to come to the village to see if he could not cure my little one, but he refused to come. He told my husband to give the medicine he gave him and if she did not get better to bring her to San Bernadino, but she is too ill to bear the journey."

When she finished her California travels, Helen sailed with her husband from San Francisco to Oregon. Visiting Washington also, they saw

Chinese laborers at work on the Northern Pacific Railway line to connect St. Paul with Puget Sound. They were impressed with the hordes of European immigrants in Seattle.

Back in Colorado Springs, Helen turned out her usual large volume of writings, but she remembered the Mission Indians and in particular Helen Sheriff's warning that the Indians at Saboba would soon face forced removal. She now wanted an official appointment in the Department of Indian Affairs, and started correspondence on the matter. Her idea was to do a careful survey of the Mission Indians. She estimated her own expenses at $1200 and promised that if the project took longer and cost more than she had anticipated, she would defray the remainder herself. In July 1882, her appointment as Special Commissioner of Indian Affairs in Southern California was approved by President Arthur. She accepted the position on the condition that Abbot Kinney be made her co-agent and interpreter. Kinney owned an estate near Sierra Madre, and Helen had met him the previous year. He spoke Spanish and had a fair knowledge of California land laws.

Knowing that she would return to California, Helen arranged with the *Independent* to write six sketches of Indian villages at $250 apiece. (Her *Century* sketches brought in $1250, were reprinted elsewhere, and as late as 1902, the public schools were using her material on Father Junipero Serra.) March 1883 found Helen in Los Angeles. She and Kinney left immediately for Saboba on learning that the Indians there had been ordered out. Kinney believed that legal action was necessary. Later they engaged a reputable Los Angeles law firm, to whom Helen personally guaranteed payment if it could be met in no other way. The *Los Angeles Express* of April 6 stated:

> Mrs. Helen Jackson has been appointed with Abbot Kinney to look into the Indian Reservations of the State and report on some plan either to protect the Indians in possession of their "Commons" or to propose some plan by which they can be distributed each on a plot of his own . . .

The investigating committee consisted of Helen, named General by Kinney; of Kinney himself, named Comrade, or Co, by Helen; of Sandham, the artist who had accompanied Helen the year before; and of Newell Harris Mitchell. The latter owned a livery stable in Anaheim and was the driver of their two-horse carriage.

The trip was not boring. Their first stop was San Juan Capistrano. From there they went south to San Diego, visiting ranches. Making San Diego their base, they made excursions to various places. They journeyed to such places as Pala, Ricon and the Temecula Valley. They visited Indians in the mountains and valleys. Sometimes it was necessary on rough trails to use ponies without shoes rather than horses. Near Warner's Springs, Kinney was able to prevent illegal seizures by two white men from the San Ysido Indians. On the way to Santa Ysabel, they were forced to stay for three days in a drafty cabin because of a spring snowstorm. They visited Los Coyotes, so inaccessible that no Indian agent had ever visited it. In one of the villages, Helen talked with a young chief named Alessandro, whose name must have come to mind as she planned *Ramona*. In one month the party visited all bands of Indians in the three southernmost counties of Southern California except for the desert Indians of Agua Caliente and the Conejos. For these Helen and Kinney had to use secondary, but reliable, reports.

At home in Colorado Springs, Helen worked up her articles and the materials for the government. Kinney, bound for New York, stopped off for a few days to do some minor editing. Their report on the conditions and needs of the Mission Indians in California was submitted to Hiram Price, Commissioner of Indian Affairs, on July 13, 1883. It contained facts and figures carefully and systematically gathered during the investigation. One sentence seems to tell it all: "From tract after tract of such lands they have been driven out, year by year, by the white settlers of the country, until they can retreat no farther, some of their villages being literally in the last tillable spot on the desert's edge or in mountain fastness." There followed 11 recommendations for bettering conditions, including one that all white settlers be removed from the reservations; the need for more schools was emphasized.

As the months passed, Helen realized that letters, interviews, her *Century of Dishonor,* even her recent report had failed to move Congress to make any significant changes. In late October the plot for a novel about Indians flashed into her mind. On November 8, 1883, she wrote to her Los Angeles friends, the Coronels:

> I am going to write a novel, in which will be set forth some Indian experiences in a way to move people's hearts. People will read a novel when they will not read serious books.... If you think of any romantic incidents, either Mexican or Indian, which would work in well into a story of Southern California, please write them out for me. I wish I had had this plan in my mind last year when I was in Los Angeles. I would have taken notes of the many interesting things you told me.

She began *Ramona* on December 1 and a month later wrote, "If I can do one-hundredth part for the Indians as Mrs. Stowe did for the Negroes, I will be thankful...."

Helen had been deeply immersed in the Indian problem ever since hearing Standing Bear and Bright Eyes speak in Boston. Writing *Ramona* appears to have been almost a compulsion, and she worked at it with singular concentration. Because of either physical or mental illness, she was forced at times to stop. To Higginson she admitted: "It racks me like a struggle with an outside power. . . . Twice, since beginning it I have broken down utterly for a week. What I have to endure in holding myself away from it, no words can tell. It is like keeping away from a lover, whose hand I can reach. . . ."

The story was to be a weekly serial in *The Christian Union,* but unlike *Uncle Tom's Cabin,* the manuscript would be finished before the appearance of the first installment. Helen read aloud most of the chapters to a woman friend whose judgment she trusted. She completed the book in March after what must have been a supreme effort. Roberts Brothers brought out *Ramona* in book form in 1884 in time for the Christmas sales. It has remained in print ever since.

Helen's famous work tells the tragic story of Alessandro Assis, the handsome Indian who is captain of a sheep-shearing band, and the beautiful convent-educated Ramona Ortega, or Majella, the daughter of a Scot and an Indian woman, but brought up by a domineering and unloving Spanish woman named Moreno. Ramona leaves her comfortable life at the fine Moreno ranch to marry Alessandro. Alessandro's prospects are poor; his people have just been driven out of Temecula, their village, and his father is dead. The couple settle in San Pasquale, and are beginning to prosper. But they have to leave as American ranchers take over the land. On the way to Saboba, they encounter a severe snowstorm. Exposure to the cold is fatal to their baby girl, Eyes-of-the-Sky, for she dies later as she is being taken to the agency doctor who has refused to come to her. As the white settlers continue to encroach, Alessandro moves his wife to a small valley high on the slopes of Mount San Jacinto. Here Ramona has a second daughter. Now Alessandro is showing signs of mental illness. One day, when "loco," he rides home on a horse that does not belong to him. As he tries to explain his error, Jim Farrer, the white owner, shoots and kills him. Gathering her baby in her arms, Ramona runs down the mountain to Cauhilla, seeking help. Here she falls ill. She is found by Felipe Moreno, whom she calls her brother and who has always loved her. When she recovers, he takes her and the baby to Mexico City. Here Ramona and Felipe are married and begin a new life.

From the novel itself, we conclude that Helen envisaged the story taking place in the 1850s. Yet the historical eviction from Temecula took place in 1875. Likewise, an Indian named Juan Diego was shot by a white man named Sam Temple in 1883. Helen used the details of the latter episode in describing the killing of Alessandro by Jim Farrer. But the fact that these and other incidents took place later does not detract from the authentic background of the story. The memories of her California experiences and her research served her well. For instance, she describes a sheep shearing based on her own observations. Here she mentions the Temecula eviction:

> "In Temecula!" exclaimed Alessandro, fiercely. "You don't seem to understand, Senorita. We have no right in Temecula, not even to our graveyard full of dead. Mr. Rothsaker warned us all not to be hanging around there; for he said the men who were coming in were a rough set, and they would shoot any Indian at sight, if they saw him trespassing on their property."
> "Their property!" ejaculated Ramona.
> "Yes, it is theirs," said Alessandro, doggedly. "That is the law. They've got all the papers to show it. That is what my father always said, — if the Senor Valdez had only given a paper! But they never did in those days. Nobody had papers. The American law is different."

Regard for the Franciscan padres is shown here as Father Salvierderra arrives at the Moreno ranch on foot.

> "Old age is conquering me. It will not be many times more that I shall see this place."
> "Oh, do not say that, Father," cried Ramona; "you can ride when it tires you too much to walk. The Senora said, only the other day, that she wished you would let her give you a horse; that it was not right for you to take these long journeys on foot. You know we have hundreds of horses. It is nothing, one horse," she added, seeing the Father slowly shake his head.
> "No," he said, "it is not that. I could not refuse anything at the hands of the Senora. But it was the rule of our order to go on foot. We must deny the flesh. Look at our beloved master in this land, Father Junipero, when he was past 80, walking from San Diego to Monterey, and all the while a running ulcer in one of his legs, for which most men would have taken to a bed, to be healed. It is a sinful fashion that is coming in, for monks to take their ease doing God's work...."
> While they were still talking, they had been slowly moving forward, Ramona slightly in advance, gracefully bending the mustard branches, and holding them down till the Father had followed her steps.

Helen's eye for color enabled her to write attractive descriptions such as this one:

> Between the veranda and the river meadows, out on which it looked, all was garden, orange grove, and almond orchard; the orange grove always green, never without snowy bloom or golden fruit; the garden never without flowers, summer or winter; and the almond orchard, in early spring, a fluttering canopy of pink and white petals, which, seen from

**Ramona and Alessandro are pictured in a scene from the Ramona Outdoor Play.
Courtesy Ramona Pageant Association.**

the hills on the opposite side of the river, looked as if rosy sunrise clouds
had fallen, and become tangled in the tree-tops. On either hand stretched
away other orchards, — peach, apricot, pear, apple, pomegranate; and
beyond these, vineyards. Nothing was to be seen but verdure or bloom
or fruit, at whatever time of year you sat on the Senora's south veranda.

In 1908 George Wharton James' book *Through Ramona's Country*
dispelled many myths about *Ramona*. Also, those who claimed to know the
original Ramona or Alessandro had to deal with this from Susan Coolidge,
a writer friend of Helen's:

On her (Mrs. Jackson's) desk that winter stood an unframed photograph,
after Dante Rosetti, — two heads, a man's and a woman's, set in a nimbus
of cloud, with a strange beautiful regard and meaning in their eyes. They
were exactly her idea of what Ramona and Alessandro looked like, she
said. The characters of the novel never, I think, came so near to
materialization in her eyes as in this photograph. It was a purely ideal
story. . . . I have no reason to suppose, from anything said by her, that she
intentionally described any exact place or person.

Helen was distressed when the *New York Times'* review referred to
Ramona as a romance. But she was elated when Emily Dickinson wrote,
"Pity me, however, I have just finished *Ramona*. Would that like

Shakespeare, it were just published." Whether Emily was sincere is open to question.

Soon after she returned to Colorado Springs in June 1884, Helen suffered a compound fracture of the hip which crippled her for life. When Emily Dickinson wrote to express her sympathy, Helen thanked her and added, "It is a cruel wrong to your 'day and generation' that you will not give them [Dickinson's poems] light. — If such a thing should happen as that I should outlive you, I wish you would make me your literary legatee & executor." As it turned out, Emily outlived Helen by a short space. Helen, regarded by some as the leading poetess in the United States, apparently recognized Emily's talent and perhaps knew that her own poems were inferior to her friend's.

Helen hoped that California would put her back on her feet again, but after she went there, she became worse. It was soon clear that she was also suffering from an emaciating disease (cancer of the stomach?). Will arrived on August 2 and she died ten days later. On August 8 she wrote to President Grover Cleveland:

> Dear Sir:
>   From my deathbed I send you message of heartfelt thanks for what you have already done for the Indians. I ask you to read my "Century of Dishonor." I am dying happier for the belief I have that it is your hand that is destined to strike the first steady blow toward lifting this burden of infamy from our country and righting wrongs of the Indian race.
>   With respect and gratitude,
>   Helen Jackson

In 1887 President Cleveland signed the Dawes Severalty Act. Humanitarian in intent, this legislation assumed the desirability of assimilating the Indian into the white culture. Essentially, it broke up tribal ownership of land by dividing the tribal reservation among individual Indians, at the same time conferring on them citizenship. In practice, the act was a failure. The social structure of the tribe was weakened; many nomadic Indians were unable to adjust to an agricultural existence and some Indians were cheated out of their property. Any "surplus" land was to be made available for sale to whites. By 1932 the latter had acquired two-thirds of the 138,000 acres held by the Indians when the act went into effect. In contrast to the philosophy behind the act, twentieth century sociologists and anthropologists stress cultural diversity rather than the melting pot concept.

In appraising Helen as an author, we should note that she was one of the successful and prolific writers of her era. Her poems were popular for many years after her death. But, according to Higginson, Helen wanted to be remembered for her *Century of Dishonor,* nonfiction based on careful research, and *Ramona,* fiction with a message. As the author of these, she used Helen Hunt Jackson, not a pen name. *Century* was out of print, but is now available again. How much *Ramona* helped the Indians is not known. It remains, however, an American classic. It has been dramatized as a stage play, and there have been movie versions. Since 1923 the Ramona Pageant Association has produced the story as an outdoor festival in Hemet, California. More than one hundred years after the book was written, thousands attend the performances given there every spring. Helen Hunt Jackson used her considerable talent to fight for a wronged people. In so doing, she produced an enduring monument to herself.

Clara Barton
American Red Cross

On March 1, 1882, President Arthur signed the Geneva Convention of 1864, and 15 days later the Senate ratified it. By this action the United States became the thirty-second nation that agreed to provide humane treatment to the wounded, whether friend or foe.

The moving force behind the treaty's acceptance was Clara Barton, then 60. With unflagging determination she had approached presidents, politicians, editors and other influential persons until victory was won.

Clarissa Harlowe Barton was born in North Oxford, Massachusetts, on Christmas Day 1821, the youngest of five children of Sarah Stone and Stephen Barton. Her father was a farmer, a Jacksonian Democrat and local political leader. Known as Captain Barton, he had fought Indians under General Anthony Wayne. This he considered a patriotic duty, and he instilled in Clara a love of country comparable to that of Emma Willard. He never tired of recounting his army adventures, and through him she developed a lifelong interest in military activities. Mrs. Barton, whose ancestors had fought in the Revolution, was a practical woman who trained her daughter to become a competent cook and housekeeper.

Clara was subjected to the common school curriculum. However, her parents and siblings — the latter all considerably older than she — apparently were responsible for much of her education. She learned to use hammer and saw, to grind and mix paints, to hang wallpaper and use putty. Put on an unbroken colt when only five and given her own Morgan horse five years later, Clara became an excellent horsewoman. Such non-academic accomplishments would serve her well in the course of her life. Although the Bartons belonged to the Universalist church, they were not liberated enough to allow their daughter to learn to dance or even skate.

When David Barton was badly injured in a barn raising, Clara, then only 11, nursed her brother for two years. This experience seems to have given her a feeling of confidence in the same way that Louisa May Alcott was inspired to care for sick and wounded Union soldiers. At 17 Clara began to teach at a district school near her family home. Although a tiny woman, she apparently had no difficulty in maintaining discipline. For the next ten years, she taught at various schools and kept books for her brothers.

Clara never married and little is known about any serious romances. She turned down one man who made his fortune in the 1849 Gold Rush, but he gave her $10,000, which remained banked for years and was used ultimately only for "good works."

Following a year of study at Liberal Institute in Clinton, New York, Clara taught in Highstown, New Jersey. Her mother had died and her aging father was living with one of her brothers, so she was not needed by her family.

With education not yet free in New Jersey, Clara started one of that state's first free public schools in Bordentown. In the beginning she worked without recompense, and only boys came. But the venture was so successful that she was soon receiving a salary. In addition, another teacher was hired and a building accommodating 600 students was made available. But Clara was dealt a blow when a male principal was installed. Apparently she could not work under him, so she resigned.

During her long life, Clara was subject to depressions that were often preceded by voice loss. Just before she left New Jersey, her vocal cords failed her. Hoping that a warm climate might improve her voice, she went to Washington, D.C., in 1854.

Here Clara found Colonel Alexander DeWitt, a Congressman from her home state and a friend of her family's. Through him she became a clerk in the Patent Office. It was her duty to make clear and accurate copy, for which she was paid 10 cents per 100 words. At first she earned from $71 to $83 a month. Judge Charles Mason, the Commissioner of Patents, found her industrious and reliable, and in time she was promoted, earning as much as $1400 a year.

The Patent Office was under the jurisdiction of Robert McClellan, President Pierce's secretary of the interior. McClellan did not believe that women should work in government offices, declaring, "There is much obvious impropriety in the mixing of the sexes within the walls of a public office, and I am determined to arrest the practice."

Despite this, Clara remained there until 1857, and after an absence, from 1860 to 1865. During the Civil War, whenever she was away from her desk, she shared her salary with Edward Shaw of Attleboro, Massachusetts, who substituted for her.

Before 1883 when the Pendleton, or Civil Service, Act became law, government positions such as Clara held depended largely on patronage. Women were not welcome in them. But the Pendleton Act finally made it possible for the first time for women to compete directly with men for positions in the federal government.

Clara's government employment was tenuous because it depended on political patronage and because she was a woman, but it appears that

Clara Harlowe Barton—circa 1882. Courtesy American Red Cross.

she was very competent at her work and that her superiors wished to retain her.

The antebellum years in Washington were especially significant for Clara Barton. Although she lived frugally in rented rooms, worked from 9 until 3 and then brought home copy to work on during the evening, she had opportunity to meet many influential persons and to learn much about the operation of the government.

Although Captain Barton favored the Democrats, his daughter was beginning to lean toward the Republican Party, despite the fact that she had no vote. She soon became acquainted with Charles Sumner, whom we met earlier. After hearing him speak on the Kansas-Nebraska Act, she termed his oration "of greater power than any I ever knew." Clara was also privileged to hear Lincoln's First Inaugural Address. There was no question of her abolitionist sympathies.

When DeWitt lost his seat in Congress, she made it a point to know Henry Wilson, the Republican senator from Massachusetts and later vice president under Grant. Wilson remained her friend and ally until his death. So when the Civil War began, Clara at 39 was self-assured and at home in Washington.

On April 19, 1861, soldiers of the Sixth Massachusetts Regiment on their way to Washington were mobbed in Baltimore while crossing from one railroad station to another. Having heard this, Clara went to the station the next day to meet these men from her native state. Among them were friends and former pupils from Worcester and North Oxford. Their baggage had been taken; they were sweltering in heavy, woolen clothing. As part of the defense plan for the capital city, the Sixth would be quartered in the Senate Chambers. The next day, Clara appeared there with five Negro porters who carried boxes of food and clothing for the soldiers. This was the beginning of her crusade to make life more comfortable for the fighting men.

Her next act was to write the Worcester *Daily Spy*, appealing for supplies and money for the Sixth. The response from sewing circles, church societies and the like was so great that she had to rent storage space for the donations.

After the death of Captain Barton in March 1862, Clara sought permission to work at the front. Of course she encountered tremendous opposition, but she persevered until she obtained the necessary military passes. She was granted free transportation by train or steamboat, but would receive no pay. Through letters and personal contacts, she was receiving many contributions; when necessary, she spent her own money for supplies.

Two days after the Battle of Cedar Mountain, close to Culpepper,

Virginia, she appeared on the scene at midnight, with a four-mule train pulling a wagon full of supplies. She had discarded her crinoline and was dressed plainly and comfortably.

According to Brigade Surgeon James L. Dunn of Pennsylvania, who was there, the men were out of dressings of every kind. He wrote, ". . . she supplied us with everything, and while the shells were bursting in every direction took her course to the hospital on our right, where she found everything wanting again. After doing all she could on the field, she returned to Culpepper, where she staid dealing out shirts to the naked wounded, and preparing soup, and seeing it prepared in all the hospitals." Dunn claimed that he was the first to call her the Angel of the Battlefield.

This sums up Clara's usefulness on the battlefield—being where she was needed when she was needed and with needed supplies. Like Florence Nightingale in the Crimean War, Clara was an organizer and she, too, soon developed a feeling for what provisions were needed, and knew how to obtain them. Another salient fact is that she was acting independently.

We saw that the Sanitary Commission was formed early in the war. Before the war ended, it had about 7000 auxiliary societies to act as "centers of collection" for the supplies of food, clothing, lint and bandages it distributed. It used experienced physicians to make investigations, supplied female nurses to Army hospitals, established "soldiers' homes" for convalescents and organized corps for aid on the battlefield. Formed at the insistence of women, most of the Sanitary Commission's supplies and money were obtained through the efforts of women who were determined to have no second Crimeas.

Although Clara had no official connection with its work, she always had a good relationship with the organization. In fact, before leaving for the scene of battle, she had obtained goods from the Sanitary Commission for distribution to the soldiers. She also maintained a good working relationship with the Christian Commission.

Unlike Louisa May Alcott, Clara made no effort to apply to Dorothea Dix for admission to her corps of nurses. Perhaps Clara knew that her own personality was such that she could not function well under Miss Dix's authority. Nevertheless, when in 1910 the New York *World* asked her for a list of eight names which she would nominate for a Women's Hall of Fame, Dorothea Dix was on Clara's list.

After the Second Battle of Bull Run was fought August 28–30, 1862, Clara arrived by train on August 31 at Fairfax Station, Virginia, with three woman helpers and supplies of bandages, drugs, coffee, brandy, wine, crackers and other edibles. She secured the help of 50 prisoners-of-war. The wounded were being brought in by the wagonload from the battlefield to the station, where trains would transport them to Washington. In a letter to a cousin, Clara described their condition.

> The men were brought down from the field and laid on the ground beside the train and so back up the hill till they covered acres. The bales of hay and forage were broken open and the ground was littered like bedding for horses. . . . By night there must have been three thousand helpless men lying in that hay. We had two water buckets—five dippers—the stores which we carried to eat besides hard crackers—my one stew pan, which I remembered to take, and this made coffee for them. All night we made compresses and slings and bound up and wet wounds when we could get water. . . .

She also mentioned fears that someone's candle would fall into the hay.

By now Clara was recognized as what her biographer Ishbel Ross terms "an army housekeeper who cooked for the men and fed them in the field." Of course she helped the surgeons, promised the dying to write letters for them and did whatever she could to improve the lot of the living. Her compassion and efficiency quickly earned the respect of many.

On September 17, 1862, Generals McClellan and Lee fought each other ferociously on the high ground above Antietam Creek, near Sharpsburg, Maryland. Before dusk almost 20,000 men were wounded in the conflict. Clara, accompanied by four men in a wagon laden with supplies, followed Burnside's cavalry and artillery until she came to a farmhouse and barn in a cornfield. The fighting had stopped in this immediate area, but there was a constant stream of wounded to attend to. The surgeons had a small amount of chloroform, but had run out of almost everything else. Since there was no hope of getting supplies until later, her stores seemed like a miracle.

Amid dense smoke and the roar of distant artillery, she got to work. A bullet hit one man she was bending over to offer a drink; with the help of one wounded man, she removed with a pen knife a bullet embedded in the jaw of another; following a doctor's instructions, she gave chloroform. By two o'clock her food supply was gone. She had brought 12 cases of wine, which were used both as a stimulant and for anesthesia. Nine cases were packed in sawdust and for some unexplainable reason, three in cornmeal. Jackson's troops had stored some barrels of Indian meal and a bag of salt in the cellar. There were large kettles in the kitchen. With the help of 30 men, Clara made hot gruel for all the men lying on the ground, and the line extended for miles. When it grew dark, four cases of lanterns brought by Clara helped the surgeons to operate. (She had not forgotten the danger of using candles near the hay at Cedar Mountain.)

Soon the Sanitary Commission was on the scene to help, and on the third day, the army's own supplies arrived. By then, Clara was exhausted. She was returned to Washington in the wagon, and it took several days for her to recover.

On December 3 Burnside crossed the Rappahannock to advance on Richmond via Fredericksburg, Virginia. Lee drove him back, causing many Union casualties. The freezing weather added to their misery. (We recall that Louisa May Alcott helped to nurse wounded brought to Washington after the battle of Fredericksburg.)

Clara was on the spot with the Rev. C.M. Welles as her helper. On the 14th, he wrote, "A shell shattered the door of the room in which she was attending to wounded men. She did not flinch but continued her duties as usual."

In the aftermath of battle, the wounded were packed into houses, hotels, tents and churches. Many had been lying in the snow for hours, among them some Confederate prisoners. As usual, Clara did whatever she could. And she did not discriminate between wounded Federals or Rebels. The men did not forget; her fame was now firmly established.

From April until December 1863, Clara was on the South Carolina coast at Hilton Head (Port Royal) and Morris Island, where Union forces were bent on taking the forts of Moultrie, Johnson, Wagner and Sumter. During this time she tended wounded Negro soldiers under the command of Col. Robert Shaw. By now the Sanitary Commission and Miss Dix's nurses were well organized, and Clara's efforts were less needed and, perhaps, less appreciated. Because she no longer felt useful to the army, she became despondent.

But when her services were requested following the Battle of Spotsylvania on May 8, 1864, her spirits revived.

A short time later, General Benjamin Butler appointed Clara Superintendent of the Department of Nurses for the Army of the James. With this title, she had more authority and assets than before. Here is her description of one day's activities. "I have had a barrel of apple sauce made today and given out every spoonful of it with my own hands. I have cooked ten dozen eggs, made cracker toast, cornstarch blanc mange, milk punch, arrow-root, washed hands and faces, put ice on hot heads, mustard on cold feet, written six soldiers' letters home, stood beside three death beds. . . ." She still received "the boxes and barrels of food and raiment" sent for distribution by grateful Americans. And in the evening, in her tent, she wrote scores of letters. Around this time, she nursed a young Swiss named Jules Golay, through whom she would one day go to Geneva.

As the ghastly Civil War came to a close, Clara turned to the tasks of tracing men missing in the conflict and also trying to locate the burial places of soldiers reported as dead. The tasks were formidable. Numerous soldiers were buried in unidentified graves; there were some 44,000 recorded deaths in excess of the number of graves; of the thousands missing, many were dead, some were deserters, some bounty-jumpers, some prisoners.

By February 1865, Clara had set up an office in Annapolis, using her own funds to pay a small work force. A month later, just before his assassination, Lincoln approved the project. Late in May the group had compiled a list of names of 3000 missing men. Andrew Johnson, now president, authorized the Government Printing Office to make copies. Arranged according to states, the names were published by newspapers in that state and posted in suitable conspicuous places. Information was requested of anyone able to furnish it. The response was overwhelming.

After a while, the War Department provided some free transportation and helped to defray the cost of stationery and postage; even a horse was placed at Clara's disposal. Later Congress appropriated $15,000 to cover the expenses involved. An accounting to Congress in 1869 showed that the project had cost $16,759.33.

Because of her work in tracing the war dead, Clara came into contact with a young Federal soldier named Dorence Atwater. Atwater had been taken prisoner by the Confederates and ultimately sent to their infamous prison at Andersonville, Georgia. Prisoners had been subjected to inhuman conditions, resulting in a horrifying death rate, with the men dying principally from scurvy and diarrheal diseases. Atwater's duty was to record the Union deaths, giving name, corps, regiment and cause of death. In addition to the official list, he made a duplicate one which he took with him when he was finally exchanged. In time Atwater approached Clara, maintaining that because the bodies were buried in the order listed, he could identify the graves corresponding to the names on the register. Clara was given permission to go to Andersonville with Atwater and a force of 40 workers, under command of an Army officer. In a few days almost 13,000 graves were marked, the grounds were enclosed and the Stars and Stripes was flying over them.

After some difficulties, Clara sought the advice of Horace Greeley in getting the rolls published. They came out in pamphlet form, with heavy advertising by Greeley's *New York Tribune*.

Clara continued this quest for missing soldiers until 1868. The work involved writing thousands of letters. In the end, she estimated that she had been able to give some 22,000 families information that they lacked. Considering the anguish of anyone with a loved one missing in action, it is clear that this was a worthwhile endeavor to which Clara gave her energy, and one that gave her valuable experience in publicity.

Between 1866 and 1868, Clara took to the lecture circuit, relating her wartime experiences. She traveled through the East and Midwest, usually earning $100 for a 90-minute talk. The venture was a great financial success and served to increase her fame. But it also had its price. One evening, when she faced an audience, her voice failed her, as it had in Bordentown. With a diagnosis of "nervous prostration," rest and a trip to Europe were prescribed for her. Fortunately, she was now financially independent and her money well-invested.

It was in Switzerland that Clara first learned of the International Red Cross. This society came into existence because of the vision of Jean Henri Dunant, a religious and idealistic Swiss. In northern Italy in 1859, Dunant had witnessed the terrible devastation caused by the Battle of Solferino, fought by Italians and French against the Austrians. One day's fighting caused 39,000 casualties. Appalled by the lack of care for the wounded of both sides, Dunant organized volunteers to help as best they could. Memories of what he saw haunted him.

Three years later in Geneva, he wrote *Un Souvenir de Solferino,* a book that inspired the Red Cross. "Could not the means be found in time of peace," he wrote, "to organize relief societies whose aim would be to provide for the wounded in time of war by volunteers of zeal and devotion, properly qualified for such work?" Dunant sent copies of his work to influential persons in Europe. The first printing of 1600 copies was so well received that a second edition was necessary a month later, with translation into several languages.

Early in 1863, Geneva's Society for Public Welfare appointed a committee to consider Dunant's plea. This committee called an international conference later in 1863. Soon delegates from 11 nations signed the Treaty of Geneva guaranteeing neutrality for the wounded and those caring for them, agreeing to facilitate the delivery of supplies and adopting as the symbol of neutrality the reverse of the Swiss flag—a red cross against a white background. Within the next two years, there were eight more signatories.

The United States was not among them. The Sanitary Commission appeared to meet the needs of the military, and isolationism was a keynote of American foreign policy. Secretary of State Seward in 1868 declared, "It has always been deemed at least a questionable policy, if not unwise, for the United States to become a party to any instrument to which there are many other parties. Nothing but the most urgent necessity should lead to a departure of this rule." After a change in administration, Henry W. Bellows, a minister and former president of the Sanitary Commission, urged participation by his country in the Geneva Convention, but was turned down by Grant's secretary of state, Hamilton Fish.

France declared war against Prussia in July 1870. At the time, Clara was in Berne, Switzerland, recuperating from her emotional breakdown.

Almost immediately she was invited by Dr. Louis Appia, one of the original founders of the International Red Cross, to take part in relief work. A call to action seemed just the medicine she needed. Within a week she was in Basel, witnessing the organization in action. She wrote:

> My first steps were to the storehouses and to my amazement I found there a larger supply than I had ever seen at any one time in readiness for the field at our own Sanitary Commission rooms in Washington, even in the fourth year of the war; and the trains were loaded with boxes and barrels pouring in from every city, town, and hamlet in Switzerland, even from Austria and northern Italy, and the trained, educated nurses stood awaiting their appointments, each with this badge upon the arm or breast, and every box, package, or barrel with a broad bright scarlet cross, which rendered it as safe and sacred from molestation (one might also say) as the bread and wine before the altar.

In contrast to the latter, "I remembered our prisons, crowded with starving men whom all the powers and pities of the world could not reach even with a bit of bread."

Clara's chief service during the Franco-Prussian War was in Strasbourg and Paris where she engaged in relief work for persons devastated by the war. Again, the experiences would benefit her work with the infant American Red Cross.

Her tasks accomplished, Clara again collapsed. She returned to her homeland as an invalid and remained so for some years. The exact nature of her illness is not known, but it appears to have been emotional.

By June 1877, Clara had obtained from Dr. Appia and President Gustave Moynier of the International Red Cross an official appointment to represent the organization in the United States. A few months later, she was writing from her home in Dansville, New York, about going to see President Hayes with regard to "an international matter pertaining to humanity." Obviously she was recovered and gearing up for activity after years of inactivity.

The next year, she wrote and distributed a pamphlet that explained the purpose of the Red Cross. She went to Washington, trying to gain the support of influential people. Then she visited President Hayes, who referred her to Secretary of State William Evarts. The latter did not see her, turning her over to the Assistant Secretary, William Seward's son. The young Seward reiterated his father's and Fish's sentiments, and Clara was forced to wait for a new administration. Meanwhile, she did all she could to acquaint the public with the Red Cross. But it was an uphill battle, and people seemed little impressed.

Clara lost no time in approaching President Garfield. On March 30, 1881, he referred her to Secretary of State James Blaine, who was sympathetic. So were Robert T. Lincoln, Secretary of War, and other cabinet members she called on. A little later there was official word that the Garfield Administration would recommend to Congress the adoption of the International Treaty. But on September 19, Garfield died after being shot by a fanatic. The treaty was unsigned.

At the urging of both Garfield and Blaine, Clara had begun to organize a National Society of the Red Cross. It was incorporated under the laws of the District of Columbia and officers were elected. When Clara invited Garfield to become the president, he declined, suggesting herself.

In the third edition of *Un Souvenir de Solferino*, Dunant suggested peacetime opportunities for relief work. Clara stressed this aspect in her pamphlet:

> . . . our southern coasts are periodically visited by the scourge of yellow fever; the valleys of the Mississippi are subject to destructive inundations; the plains of the West are devastated by insects and drought, and our cities and country are swept by consuming fires. In all such cases, to gather and dispense the profuse liberality of our people, without waste of time or material, requires the wisdom that comes of experience and permanent organization.

Since war in the United States was considered remote, there was a strong possibility that peacetime relief could have strong appeal. This would necessitate the formation of local chapters. After President Garfield's shooting, Clara returned to Dansville, and on August 22, 1881, she organized the first local Red Cross Society in the United States. It was in existence until she made Washington her headquarters.

Shortly after President Arthur's inauguration, Clara returned to Washington to lay the groundwork necessary to persuade him to pursue the course that Garfield had promised to take. The new president assured this persevering woman of his support.

In 1881 Clara revised her pamphlet. This time there was widespread interest among the press, and in turn the public. When a disastrous forest fire occurred in Michigan that summer, President Barton appealed for help in the name of the new organization. Dansville, Rochester and Syracuse responded. For the first time, the nation witnessed the usefulness of the society's peacetime relief work.

After 17 years of indifference, the Senate ratified the Geneva Convention on March 16, 1882. This was a personal triumph for Clara, who had foresight that the majority of her countrymen lacked. Her steadfast determination had prevailed over opposition and apathy.

In Dansville Clara had met a young man named Julia Hubbell. When the Michigan fire broke out, he was studying medicine at Ann Arbor. She wired him to assess the situation for her. This was the beginning of Dr. Hubbell's association with the Red Cross. Until 1904 he worked as Clara's capable and trusted colleague.

For the next 23 years, Clara's name and the Red Cross were inseparable. One of the early major relief operations took place in 1884 during the Ohio and Mississippi floods. On February 15 in Cincinnati, the Ohio River rose to 70 feet, making 7000 families homeless. Homes and barns were ruined, livestock drowned and crops destroyed. The federal government allocated money, but there was plenty for the Red Cross to do. Through the newspapers, Clara made a nationwide appeal for help. With headquarters first in Cinicnnati and later at Evansville, Indiana, she chartered a river steamer and supervised the distribution of supplies. A second steamer sailed from St. Louis to New Orleans, supplying provisions en route. During four months of operation, Clara distributed supplics amounting to some $175,000.

On April 3 an editorial in the *Evansville Daily Journal* stated: "The Red Cross has become a grand educator, embodying the best principles of social science, and that true spirit of charity which counts it a privilege to serve one's fellowmen in time of trouble. The supplying of material wants—of food, raiment or shelter, is only a small part of its ministry."

Later, when Clara attended the International Red Cross in Geneva, she saw to it that an "American Amendment" was added to the constitution. This empowered the organization to provide relief in non-war disasters.

The Johnstown flood provided another opportunity for the Red Cross to be of significant service. On May 31, 1889, without warning, a dam on the Conemaugh River, located about 18 miles from Johnstown, Pennsylvania, collapsed, releasing 20,000 tons of water. On June 5, Clara, then 68, arrived with 50 Red Cross workers on the first train to get through. A number of nurses and doctors were also sent by the local Philadelphia society, one of the ever-growing number now springing up. The Red Cross remained in the area for five months, distributing supplies and housing materials worth about $200,000, and incurring other expenses amounting to $39,000.

When at last the temporary buildings for the homeless could be torn down, some of the lumber was shipped to Washington to become eventually a headquarters for the Red Cross and a home for Clara in Glen Echo, Maryland.

Not everyone approved of the type of help rendered after the flood; some criticized Clara for helping "the shiftless." This probably reflected the prevailing attitude about the work ethic, but Clara did learn with experience. Later she wrote: "But there is always a right time for any benevolent work to cease; a time when the community is ready to resume its own burdens, and when an offered charity is an insult to the honest and independent, and a degradation to the careless and improvident. . . ."

On August 27, 1893, the Sea Islands, off the coast of South Carolina, suffered a severe hurricane that left 30,000 people starving, most of whom were Negroes. With no government aid appropriated, President Cleveland and the governor of South Carolina appealed to the Red Cross. Assembling a corps of volunteers, Clara set up headquarters at Beaufort. She visited the cabins of victims, formed sewing circles, handed out tools, seeds and garments; as usual, whatever her hand found to do, was done with her might. Her program especially stressed rehabilitation; ten months later, houses had been rebuilt, ditches dug, gardens replanted and a good cotton crop was expected.

The American Red Cross was in Galveston following a hurricane and tidal wave in 1900. It assisted in international relief: the Russian famine in 1892 and the Armenian massacres in Turkey in 1896. In 1898 an attempt was made to help victims of the Cuban insurrection against Spain. In a very short time, the Spanish-American War broke out. Here would be a test for the new organization.

It should be appreciated that local Red Cross societies had rather a loose connection with the national body. Before the war ended, the New York City group, which was by far the strongest of the local societies, had provided almost 700 nurses for army hospitals. By now professional nursing was coming into its own, and the military was beginning to recognize the value of trained nurses.

Despite her age, Clara was in the thick of things. Aboard the *State of Texas,* she had intended to have its cargo used for the relief of Cuban refugees. But now the Red Cross staff was ordered to aid the American sick and wounded. After the vessel was unloaded, the supplies were packed into two six-mule army wagons and transported to the front. Behind them in a third wagon rode the 76-year-old Clara Barton. An army surgeon described the conditions she found:

> The surgical force in this hospital was insufficient to meet the demands made upon it, and numbers of the wounded lay unattended for twelve and even twenty-four hours before their turn came. There was an insufficient supply of proper food for invalids, due to the lack of transportation. . . . Another great want was the scarcity of clothing and blankets. . . . Men were often taken from the operating table and of necessity in many cases were laid upon the wet ground without shelter, and in the majority of cases without even a blanket, and with little or no nourishment for two awful days, until the Red Cross Society, under Miss Barton, appeared on the scene.

When she had done what she could for the wounded, Clara turned her attention to feeding the starving people of Santiago. The Red Cross Committee in New York sent additional supplies after everything remaining in the *State of Texas* had been used. About 6000 tons of goods, costing some $500,000, were dispensed by the Red Cross in the Cuban operation.

Obviously Clara could not run the American Red Cross forever, although in 1902 her supporters had railroaded changes in the by-laws to give their 80-year-old favorite the title of president for life. It was becoming increasingly clear that better management and accountability were needed. As Clara's battlefield service had been a reflection of her own individuality, so were her Red Cross relief operations. To insure prompt action, she insisted on distributing some funds at her own discretion. But after the Galveston disaster, the Board of Control ruled that "all moneys for the American National Red Cross shall be paid to the Treasurer directly and shall be disbursed by him directly. . . ." There was also a feeling among many that the organization needed younger blood, and that Clara, who had become somewhat domineering and inflexible, should step down.

The opposition to Barton was led by an able woman named Mabel Boardman. Her forces objected to the new by-laws and instigated a Congressional investigation of the Red Cross. They objected to "the method of administration and the personal character of business management, which had caused loss of public confidence." The investigation disclosed that a farm in Indiana had been deeded to Clara, as president of the American Red Cross, supposedly for a token payment of $1. The Boardman group contended that $12,000 had been paid by Clara through the diversion of funds originally raised for relief. Clara's bookkeeping was admittedly sloppy, but the Boardman forces were never able to prove their point. In the midst of the investigation, Clara submitted her resignation in 1904. Miss Boardman continued her vendetta against Clara. She tried to discredit her opponent's battlefield image, and even after Clara's death in 1912, wrote, "Her connection with the Red Cross is like a skeleton in the closet upon which the doors have been closed."

Under Miss Boardman the organization prospered. In contrast to Clara, she remained in Washington to concentrate on obtaining support and resources necessary for effective relief. World War I and II provided opportunities for expanded services and recognition. The organization's provision for blood and plasma for the armed services during the Second World War was truly outstanding. Today, the American Red Cross is an organization with more than 20,000 staff members and 1.5 million service volunteers. Nationally, it provides services to members of the armed services and veterans, aids disaster victims, annually collects more than 6 million units of blood, trains more than 2 million individuals in CPR each year and gives instruction in first aid, home nursing and the like. Internationally, it provides relief whenever there is urgent need. (In 1985, $21 million, earmarked for famine relief, was raised in a few months.)

Foreign governments decorated Clara, but it was not until 1976 that she was elected to the Hall of Fame for Great Americans, over Boardman's earlier objection. A 3-cent stamp in honor of her and the American Red Cross was issued in 1948.

Besides her leadership role in the Red Cross, Clara was interested in prison reform and temperance. She was also a supporter of the suffrage movement, although she was not as active in it as feminists Susan B. Anthony and Lucy Stone would have liked. On the lecture circuit she was once advertised as one who would not lecture on women's rights "after the style of Susan B. Anthony and her clique. . . ." Her lecture finished, Clara said, "[T]hat paragraph, my comrades, does worse than to misrepresent me as a woman; it maligns my friend. It abuses the highest and bravest work ever done in this land for either you or me. You glorify the women who made their way to the front to reach you in your misery, and nurse you back to life. You call us angels. Who opened the way for women to go and make it possible?" She went on to say that they should bless Susan B. Anthony, Elizabeth Cady Stanton, Frances D. Gage and their followers.

Considering the prejudice against women in government, the fact that Clara was successful in obtaining and holding her position as clerk-copyist for so long was in itself a step forward in women's economic progress.

Clara's weaknesses were apparent: her tendency to emotional breakdown, her failure to delegate responsibilities and finally her lack of judgment in refusing for so long to turn over the reins of the American Red Cross to younger hands. Despite these, she was a woman of vision and action who unselfishly used her talents on behalf of mankind. Charles Sumner's appraisal is apt: "Clara Barton has the brain of a statesman, the command of a general, and the heart and hand of a woman."

Katharine Lee Bates
"America the Beautiful"

This is the story of the woman who made the phrase "from sea to shining sea" part of American culture.

Born in Falmouth, Massachusetts, on August 12, 1859, Katharine Lee Bates was the fifth child of William and Cornelia (Lee) Bates. Her father was a Congregational minister, educated at Middlebury College, where his father was once president. Her mother was a graduate of Mary Lyon's Mount Holyoke Female Seminary and had taught school before she married.

Katie, as she was called, arrived only a month before her father died from a tumor. She was named for her Aunt Catherine Lee, but with a different spelling for the first name.

Mrs. Bates had a small yearly pension from the Massachusetts Congregational Society with which to bring up two surviving sons and two daughters. She managed well and supplemented her income by sewing, selling eggs and poultry and by working at home tying price tags for the Dennison Manufacturing Company. Her brothers and brother-in-law contributed what they could.

Though not on a railroad line, Falmouth was a port for sailing ships. Many of the residents were seafaring men who sailed the ocean and brought back to their village visions of a broader world. Long after it happened, Katharine recalled a sea captain who returned from Boston by stage, bringing with him a newspaper that told of Lincoln's assassination. The sea left a lasting impression on her; as a youngster in Falmouth, she could not know, of course, that one day a Liberty ship would be named for her.

Katharine's life in this Cape Cod atmosphere was secure and happy, despite the family's financial struggle. She was nearsighted and chubby; she was also imaginative and endowed with a sense of humor. These characteristics—both physical and mental—remained with her all her life.

Early in the 1870s, Mrs. Bates moved her family to Wellesley Hills so she could care for her ailing sister, Catherine Lee. But Katharine loved Falmouth and returned there for visits throughout life. Her ashes were brought there in accordance with her wishes. Today the home that was occupied by the Bates family during the first 12 years of her life is a museum

Katharine Lee Bates—1895. Courtesy Wellesley College.

known as the Katharine Lee Bates House. It contains memorabilia of those 12 years as well as some from her later life. After Katharine's death, one of her former students presented to the Falmouth Free Library a collection of her famous teacher's books.

After the move from Falmouth, Katharine attended Needham High School, graduating in 1874. Following the death of her sister, Mrs. Bates moved again, this time to Newtonville, where Katharine went to Newton High School to prepare for the new Wellesley College.

The founder of this institution was Henry Fowle Durant, a successful lawyer and astute businessman who by conversion was an evangelical Christian. Durant was first received at Mount Holyoke as a lay preacher, but later became one of its trustees in 1867. Convinced that the nation would greatly benefit if its teachers were women who had been brought to Christ, he believed that higher education for women spelled revolt — "revolt against the slavery in which women are held by the customs of society."

Durant and his wife, Pauline, had lost their young son and heir in 1863, and wished to establish a substantial memorial in his name. Rejecting his original idea of an orphanage, Durant in 1870 petitioned the Massachusetts legislature for a charter for Wellesley Female Seminary. He chose five of his original eight trustees from the Mount Holyoke board, setting the tone for the new institution. An important departure was the appointment of Pauline to the board. (Mount Holyoke, in contrast, did not have a woman board member until 1884.)

Hammett Billings was the architect of College Hall, Wellesley's 4-story main building. He designed a beautiful edifice in a nature setting of 300 acres of hills, woods and meadows and Lake Waban. Since the president and faculty were to be women, they could live in College Hall rather than in a separate house and apartments, as would be supplied for men. There were 350 rooms, each providing for two students. The building had steam heat, gas lighting and even an elevator. Durant had a decided eye for beauty, and the furnishings were tasteful and sometimes even luxurious. Unfortunately this magnificent building was destroyed by fire in 1914.

Durant, who seemed to have an endless supply of money to finance the project, kept tabs on the workmen. He forbade them to swear and he handed out Bibles for their improvement. Pauline Durant took a keen interest in the building and gave much advice. By 1873 the new seminary's name had been changed to Wellesley College. According to its statue, it "was founded for the glory of God and the service of the Lord Jesus Christ, in and by the education and culture of women." It also required "that every Trustee, Teacher, and Officer, shall be a member of an Evangelical Church, and that the study of the Holy Scriptures shall be pursued by every student throughout the entire college course under the direction of the Faculty."

A faculty of 30 was desired. When Durant realized it would be difficult to obtain so many qualified female instructors, he arranged for promising young women to get the necessary training.

So the Wellesley that Katharine entered as a freshman in 1876 was essentially not unlike Mount Holyoke; here too were high academic standards and strict discipline; furthermore, an hour of light domestic work was required for each student.

Katharine's expenses were paid by her elder brother, Arthur Lee Bates. Realizing that his sister had the makings of a scholar, he generously paid out of his annual salary of $1200 from an insurance company the $250 required to cover tuition and room and board for a year at Wellesley. Katharine entered the new college a year after its founding, graduating with 42 other members of the class of 1880. Arthur had made a good investment — his sister obtained a broad education, with special emphasis on English and Greek. And during these college years she gained experience in writing poetry.

Unfortunately, Katharine's brother was not allowed to attend the graduation because of a rule that barred men unless they were parents or guardians. After he learned that Pauline Durant had been permitted to have some Harvard students as her guests at the ceremony, he never forgave Wellesley.

After short stints of teaching at lower levels, Katharine took a position in the English department of her alma mater. She would remain there until her retirement in 1925. She served as chairman from 1891 until 1920, and under her leadership, Wellesley's English department earned an enviable reputation. Today Wellesley College has some 2000 students and is known internationally. Katharine was one of many dedicated women who helped Durant's institution to its position of educational importance.

Katharine herself became an accomplished writer and poet, producing learned works, reviews, children's works, books about foreign lands and, above all, poems. This literary output brought additional income. Dorothy Burgess, Katharine's biographer and the daughter of Arthur Bates, states, "Poetry was her natural mode of expression, and into it she poured her grief, her uncertainties, and her longings." She was soon regarded as a leading American poet of her day.

Three institutions recognized Katharine's scholarship by awarding her honorary degrees: Middlebury College, Oberlin College and on retirement, her own Wellesley College. It is worth noting that almost a century before Middlebury conferred the degree, Emma Willard could not study there because she was a woman. As a matter of fact, Katharine had even lectured on Shakespearean plays at Middlebury College's Bread Loaf Summer School.

Katharine was a lover of nature; she enjoyed solitude and often took long walks. She liked to travel; over the years she went abroad several times and in addition spent her sabbaticals in foreign countries. In England she studied at Oxford but toured the countryside and visited numerous historic sites. She toured continental Europe and spent some time in Spain. She visited the Holy Land and Egypt, but no matter how enjoyable her sojourns on foreign soil and how much Old-World culture she absorbed, she was always eager to return to the land of her birth.

It is interesting to compare Katharine's route to education with that pursued by Mary Lyon. The latter studied at several schools and even with individuals to learn what she wanted. In Katharine's time the education of women was sufficiently advanced that Katharine learned what she needed in the four-year course at one college. Travel and study abroad were postgraduate opportunities she was fortunate to have available to her.

The following was written when Katharine was abroad in 1890. It expresses a favorite and recurring theme of hers, not unlike Robert Browning's idea that a man's reach should exceed his grasp:

Dream and Deed

What of the deed without the dream? A song
   Reft of its music, and a scentless rose.
Except the heart outsoar the hand, the throng
   Will bless thee little for thy labor-throes.

The dream without the deed? Dawn's fairy gold,
   Paled, ere it wake the hills, to misty gray,
Except the hand obey the heart, behold
   The grieved angel turns his face away.

In 1893 Colorado College in Colorado Springs (this was Helen Hunt Jackson's home after her second marriage) invited Katharine, then 34, to lecture at its summer session. The opportunity prompted the writing of "America the Beautiful." But of course the spirit of the poem came from her life experiences.

Her first stop was Chicago, where she spent some time at the World's Columbian Exposition, or Chicago Fair. It commemorated—one year late—the four hundredth anniversary of Christopher Columbus' discovery of America. Occupying 600 acres, the White City, as it was called, was illuminated by electricity and consisted of 150 buildings of various styles of architecture. These grand, white structures were symbolic of an optimistic future for America. The architect, Daniel H. Burnham, was known for his slogan, "Make no little plans." This philosophy must have appealed to Katharine, for it was close to her own. When she wrote the lines *Thine alabaster cities gleam, Undimmed by human tears!* she obviously had in mind the White City.

She continued her trip west. A diary entry read, "Fertile prairies. Hot run across western Kansas." At her destination she saw "the purple range of the Rockies."

Later she joined a group going in a prairie wagon to the top of Pike's Peak. She wrote, "Our sojourn on the peak remains in memory hardly more than one ecstatic gaze. It was then and there, as I was looking out over the sea-like expanse of fertile country spreading away so far under those ample skies, that the opening lines of the hymn floated into my mind."

Before Katharine left Colorado for Massachusetts, she had finished "America the Beautiful." Two years passed before it was published in *The Congregationalist* on July 4, 1895. Originally the first stanza ended with:

America! America!
God shed His grace on thee
Till souls wax fair as earth and air
and music-hearted sea!

Also, "spacious" skies were once "halcyon" and the "fruited" plain was "enameled." A revised version appeared on November 19, 1904, in the *Boston Transcript*. Later changes in the opening quatrain of the third stanza were made. It had been:

O beautiful for heroes proved
In liberating strife,
Who more than self their country loved,
And mercy more than life!

The final version is the one given here. To protect against alterations, Katharine retained the copyright, but she never charged for use of the hymn after she received payment from *The Congregationalist*.

America the Beautiful

O beautiful for spacious skies,
For amber waves of grain,
For purple mountain majesties
Above the fruited plain!
America! America!
God shed His grace on thee,
And crown thy good with brotherhood
From sea to shining sea!

O beautiful for pilgrim feet,
Whose stern, impassioned stress
A thoroughfare for freedom beat
Across the wilderness!
America! America!
God mend thine every flaw,
Confirm thy soul in self-control,
Thy liberty in law!

O beautiful for glorious tale
O liberating strife,
When valiantly for man's avail,
Men lavished precious life!
America! America!
May God thy gold refine,
Till all success be nobleness,
And every gain divine!

> O beautiful for patriot dream
>> That sees beyond the years
> Thine alabaster cities gleam
>> Undimmed by human tears!
>> America! America!
> God shed his grace on thee,
> And crown thy good with brotherhood
>> From sea to shining sea!

Official version.

By 1926 the past presidents' assembly of the National Federation of Music Clubs was running a contest to find a good musical setting for the poem. Although some 900 entries were considered, none was chosen. A composition by Will C. McFarlane of Portland, Maine, was widely used.

Today "America the Beautiful" is set to the tune "Materna," which is associated with the hymn "O Mother Dear, Jerusalem." It is not known who first joined Katharine's masterpiece with "Materna," but it is an excellent match. The earliest printing of the combination was in *Fellowship Hymns,* edited by Clarence A. Barbour and published in 1910 by the Young Men's Christian Association Press. The composer of "Materna" was Samuel A. Ward of Newark, N.J., an organist, choirmaster and music dealer. He died in 1903, so it is unlikely that he knew that his setting was being used for a very popular patriotic poem.

From the beginning, the poem was well received. During the 1920s there was even a movement to have it declared the national anthem. (By act of Congress in 1931, "The Star Spangled Banner," long used by the armed services, became the official national anthem.)

On the popularity of "America the Beautiful," Katharine herself later commented, "That the hymn has gained, in these twenty-odd years, such a hold as it has upon our people, is clearly due to the fact that Americans are at heart idealists, with a fundamental faith in human brotherhood." Two members of Katharine's profession who have since commented on the work are Jacob M. Ross and Robert P. Ellis. In *Adventures in Literature* (1927), Ross wrote, "This lyric depicts the beauty of our land and presents in a glowing light those American ideals and aspirations which have helped to make our country what it is today." More than half a century after Ross, Ellis wrote:

> It radiates idealism and unabashed sentiment of a sort that has rendered so many late 19th-century poems, including many of Bates's own, unfashionable in our time, but its combination of eulogy and challenge, venerable tradition and lyric freshness, religious affirmation and spiritual admonition, has kept it alive in a more skeptical age. Set to Ward's music,

it has the further advantage of falling within the range of untrained and untalented voices. It will not soon lose its hold on us.

Katharine knew the grandeur and strength of her native land; realizing its weaknesses, she dreamed that her beloved America would become greater still. The hymn's continuing popularity attests to the fact that millions of Americans agree with her; some still press for it to be made the national anthem.

Since an individual's written expression is often a mirror of himself, we shall look at some of Katharine's characteristics.

While she was being considered for the position of department chairman, the Wellesley trustees were contemplating making a theological requirement of faculty members. As we have seen, the original statutes required teachers to belong to an Evangelical church. However, by 1890 this was not being enforced well enough to suit some trustees. Although Durant was now dead, there was a push to restore the original religious emphasis. Proposed amendments required, for example, "sympathy with Evangelical views as commonly held by Protestant churches." From letters written by Katharine when she was on leave to study in Europe, we know that she was prepared to resign should a restrictive amendment be adopted. To her mother she stated, ". . . I do not think it right for a college which is established to seek truth, to dictate its truth at the onset." Later she wrote, "If Wellesley cannot tell from my life and teaching of the past years whether I am a Christian or not, I do not find it in me to make lip-protestations, especially when there is a Professorship to be gained by it." Fortunately the Board adopted an amendment suggesting that teachers be of a "decided Christian character and influence." This Katharine could in conscience accept, and she stayed on the faculty.

There was an especially close relationship between Katharine and her mother, perhaps because one had never had a father or a husband, while the other had lost her husband long ago. Here is an excerpt from a letter written by Mrs. Bates when Katharine sailed for Europe the first time:

> I am in constant remembrance of your dutiful attentions to me in a thousand ways — and wherever you are on land or sea — in this world or in another you will always be my own cherished well-beloved child, who came to me when it seemed as if life's star had set, and who has been a sunbeam always since you came.

Katharine always cherished that letter.

Mrs. Bates lived part of the time in Portland, Maine, which was Arthur's home, and the rest of the time in Wellesley. She took great interest in her daughter's doings, sewed for her, and even studied Spanish with her, becoming proficient enough to translate some short stories which they planned to publish.

Katharine's sister Jeannie had been a school teacher, but when increasing deafness forced her to resign, she became Katharine's typist. As time went on, she became financially dependent on her professor-sister. Incidentally, Katharine had a voluminous correspondence to attend to and she was a prolific writer who certainly needed secretarial assistance. Jeannie became proficient at lip-reading, and Katharine made every effort to prevent her from being shut out from what was going on.

Gone now were the days when faculty members were required to live on campus with the students. By 1907 Katharine had a comfortable and charming home of her own, built under Arthur's supervision. She named it *The Scarab*. There were rooms for her mother and sister and her friend of many years, Katharine Coman, who headed the Economics department. Another household member was Sigurd, a collie. Unfortunately, Mrs. Bates was not able to enjoy the new environment for very long; she died in January 1908. Their mother's death brought the sisters closer than ever, and Jeannie lived in Katharine's home until her death in 1928. Miss Coman remained too, but died 14 years earlier.

In 1922 Katharine wrote *Yellow Clover: A Book of Remembrance*, a collection of poems in memory of Katharine Coman. Judith Schwartz, an authority on women's history, claimed in 1979 that it is obvious "from the yearning desire that glows throughout the poems in *Yellow Clover*" that there was a homosexual relationship between the two. The reader will have to decide whether the book provides a firm basis for such an assertion.

To Arthur Katharine attributed her successes; it was he who had sacrificed to give her an education, and she always remembered it. She was in constant touch with his children and grandchildren. She dedicated her last collection of verse, *America the Dream,* to him, writing on the title page, "Where there is no vision, the people perish."

Katharine also kept in touch with her brother Sam. Here is an excerpt from a letter she once wrote him from England. She could not lose weight, she informed him. "You know our father used to say that it is 'the manifest destiny of the Bateses to be fat' and, judging from Uncle William, we can't look to the Lees for deliverance. But one day we shall be nothing but souls, and then I expect to be, as Mother predicts of Jeannie, 'a very slim angel.'" Thus it is clear that her family was an integral part of her life. This is very important, because life in all-female college community could at times be rather confining, to say nothing of demanding.

Katharine's position, of course, kept her in close contact with colleagues in the academic world and the many students who sought advice about both their futures and their personal problems. In fact, *The Scarab* was filled with such people most of the time, for she had many devoted women friends and was popular with students. Many of the literary personages of the day, Julia Ward Howe among them, were invited to Wellesley by Katharine, who wanted the college community to benefit from hearing such people. Katharine loved her work and Wellesley College, but she was fortunate in having a family that could provide her with a different sort of atmosphere.

Few persons of Katharine's day were liberals. But she was not a prejudiced person. Describing to Arthur her experiences at Oberlin College when she received an honorary degree in 1916, she wrote: "It's the most democratic place in the country, I believe, for it gave its chief honors to a negro (the new head of Tuskegee) and a Jew (that splendid Morganthau), and the commencement orator was a Cambridge Unitarian!" Many of her friends were socialists, Katharine Coman in particular, and she had much exposure to socialism's proponents. Naturally conservative, she favored capitalism. With regard to religion, she rejected dogma. A student of the New Testament, she believed in the divinity of Christ and took heart in His commandment "that ye love one another." She was shocked by the Catholic anti–Protestant activity that she saw in Spain.

After hearing Woodrow Wilson, then president of Princeton University, speak at Harvard in 1909, Katharine became his devotee. She was so impressed that she bet a male friend that Wilson would one day be president. Her hopes for peace rested on him, but when war came, she did not agree with pacifists.

So we see that the lofty sentiments expressed in "America the Beautiful" came from a thoughtful woman with high ideals. Katharine was a successful woman who was grateful to her country.

Katharine died on March 28, 1929. She of course rightly occupies a prominent place in the history of Wellesley College. Those who despair the slow progress in obtaining equal rights for the sexes should take heart in the record for women's education; when Katharine became a professor at Wellesley, less than a century had passed since Emma Willard had addressed the New York legislature on behalf of female education.

Not only Wellesley honored Katharine's memory—money was raised by public subscription to erect in Boston's Fenway a memorial tablet to her. Above the first stanza of "America the Beautiful" is the inscription "Scholar, Patriot, Poet who gave enduring speech to the love of Americans for America."

Today she is remembered for "America the Beautiful," and the rest of her poetry is forgotten. But surely she would take comfort from the words of writer Gamaliel Bradford, her contemporary: "To have put the expression of the highest and deepest patriotism into the mouths of a hundred million Americans is a monument so noble and so enduring that it seems as if no poet could possibly ask or expect anything more complete."

Epilogue

It is interesting to consider why these women, in contrast to most of their contemporaries, produced enduring monuments. Several factors, both personal and societal, seem to have figured in their successes.

Was singular determination a factor? For Emma Willard, Mary Lyon, Harriet Beecher Stowe, Clara Barton and Helen Hunt Jackson it was. On the other hand, Julia Ward Howe, Emma Lazarus and Katharine Lee Bates aspired to literary heights in poetry rather than specific composition; Louisa May Alcott was determined to be a writer but had no particular interest in writing a book for girls.

Did religion — so important in nineteenth-century United States — play a role? Certainly it was part and parcel of the lives of Lyon and Stowe and very important to Willard, Howe and Bates. For the other four, it appears to have been less dominating.

How important was opportunity? Howe and Lazarus came from privileged backgrounds. Stowe and Alcott lacked material wealth before their successes, but both had famous fathers. Willard, Lyon, Jackson, Barton and Bates were the products of substantial families of Anglo-Saxon descent — the type of family that was respected and considered the backbone of the nation. Bates, in particular, owed her college education to the generosity of a brother. All the women were of course shaped by the times in general and also specific events. But chance opportunity visited some in particular. The slavery issue was very much in the forefront when Stowe wrote *Uncle Tom;* an inspirational poem such as the "Battle Hymn" had special meaning when the country was convulsed by a civil war; the International Red Cross demonstrated to Barton the desirability of an American Red Cross; the Statue of Liberty needed an expression of its existence, and Lazarus supplied the need. For these women, Pasteur's observation that chance favors the prepared mind seems to apply. On the other hand, when Jackson tried to present to the country the wrongs done the Indian, the time was not right; it was the artistry of *Ramona* that made it an enduring contribution.

Related to opportunity is marriage, but it deserves separate mention. It could be a definite asset, it could make little difference or it could prove a disadvantage. Willard seems to have combined successfully her teaching career and her role as a wife and mother. However, she had only one child — and this was most unusual in her time. Stowe had a large family and her husband was supportive of her writing. But it should be remembered that her sister Catherine ran the Stowe household while much of *Uncle Tom's Cabin* was being written. Harriet's ability to identify with the slave mother was an asset, and it is likely that her greatest novel would have been less effective had its author not been a wife and mother. Howe had a large family and loved her children dearly, but her tenacity in following her interests in literature and philosophy caused strain in her relationship with her husband and with some of her children. She never resolved her problem, and on the surface, marriage seems to have encumbered her career. However, she may not have become an abolitionist without Chev; it is even possible that the "Battle Hymn" would never have been written had she not been his wife. Jackson began to write after she became a widow, and she insisted on continuing her career after her second marriage. Her husband seemed to agree to this, but they were apart much of the time. Her two children by Hunt died when they were young, and she was in her forties when she married Jackson. Whether or not the marriage was successful is not known. It is possible that married or single, she would have written *Ramona*. The same applies to Alcott, Lazarus, and Bates with regard to their masterpieces. As a married woman with a family, Mary Lyon would probably have had great difficulty in making a success of Mount Holyoke. Barton's activities would surely have been restricted by marriage — she herself believed she could do far more for others by remaining single.

So much for differences. These women shared in common ability and talent. Willard, Lyon and Barton certainly possessed unusual organizational ability and combined it with vision. The talents of Stowe, Alcott and Jackson earned them considerable amounts of money. Bates lived fairly comfortably on the combined earnings of her professorship and her writing. Howe became an acclaimed speaker, and Lazarus was considered a personage in the intellectual circles of her day

Finally they were noted for independence of thought and action. Willard as far back as 1819 did not shrink from asking the New York state legislature to appropriate funds for female education; without money or influence, Lyon embarked on a personal campaign to obtain an institution of higher learning for women; Stowe, a harried mother of six, considered it her duty as a Christian to paint slavery in its true colors; Howe persevered in publishing poetry in the face of criticism from her husband and sometimes scant encouragement from editors; Alcott refused to write for an editor who would have paid her more had she been a man; Lazarus used the public press to write about discrimination against Jews; when Jackson's *Century of Dishonor* failed to produce the desired result, she wrote another book, *Ramona*.

It is remarkable that these nine women, most of whom were active in the Victorian age, when woman's role was passive, have left so much that is now part of everyday American life. They and their enduring monuments should be a source of inspiration and encouragement to twentieth-century women.

Bibliography

Louisa May Alcott

Anthony, Katharine S. *Louisa May Alcott.* First published 1938; reprinted by Greenwood, 1977.

Bedell, Madelon. *The Alcotts: Biography of a Family.* New York: Clarkson Potter, 1980.

Cheney, Ednah Dow. *Louisa May Alcott: Her Life, Letters, and Journals.* Boston: Roberts Bros., 1889.

Elbert, Sarah. *A Hunger for Home: Louisa May Alcott and Little Women.* Philadelphia: Temple, 1984.

Mac Donald, Ruth K. *Louisa May Alcott.* Boston: G.K. Hall, 1983.

Meigs, Cornelia. *Invincible Louisa: The Story of the Author of Little Women.* Boston: Little, Brown, 1968.

Payne, Alma J. *Louisa May Alcott: A Reference Guide.* Boston: G.K. Hall, 1980.

Rosterberg, Leona. "Some Anonymous and Pseudonymous Thrillers of Louisa M. Alcott." *Bibliographical Society of America Papers,* **37** (1943): 131–40.

Saxon, Martha. *Louisa May: A Modern Biography of Louisa May Alcott.* Boston: Houghton Mifflin, 1977.

Stern, Madeleine B. "Louisa Alcott's Feminist Letters." *Studies in the American Renaissance,* 1978, pp. 429–52.

_____. *Louisa May Alcott.* Norman: University of Oklahoma, 1950; 2nd. ed. rev., 1971.

_____. (ed.). *Behind a Mask: The Unknown Thrillers of Louisa May Alcott.* New York: Morrow, 1975.

Talbot, Marion. "Glimpses of the Real Louisa May Alcott." *New England Quarterly,* **II** (1938): 731–38.

Ullom, Judith C. (ed.). *Louisa May Alcott: An Annotated, Selected Bibliography.* Library of Congress, 1969.

Clara Barton

Baker, Ross K. "Entry of women into federal job world—at a price." *Smithsonian.* **8,** no. 4, 1977, 82–83.

Barton, W.E. *Life of Clara Barton, Founder of the American Red Cross,* 2 vols. First published 1922; reprinted by AMS, 1969.

Brooks, Stewart. *Civil War Medicine.* Springfield IL: Thomas, 1966.

Dulles, F.R. *American Red Cross, A History.* First published 1950; reprinted by Greenwood, 1971.

Gilbo, Patrick F. *The American Red Cross: The First Century.* New York: Harper, 1981.

Hurd, Charles. *The Compact History of the American Red Cross.* New York: Hawthorne, 1959.

McElroy, John. *This Was Andersonville.* Roy Meredith (ed.). New York: McDowell, Obolensky, 1957.

Ross, Ishbel. *Angel of the Battlefield; The Life of Clara Barton.* New York: Harper, 1956.

Sears, S.W. *Landscape Turned Red: The Battle of Antietam.* New York: Ticknor and Fields, 1983.

Wilson, D.C. *Stranger and Traveler.* Boston: Little, Brown, 1975.

Woodham-Smith, C. *Florence Nightingale.* London: McGraw, 1951.

Katharine Lee Bates

Burgess, Dorothy Whittemore. *Dream and Deed: The Story of Katharine Lee Bates.* Norman: University of Oklahoma, 1952.

Ellis, Robert P. "1893 and 1983." *America:* **149** (1983), 10–12.

Fuld, James B. *The Book of World Famous Music. Classical, Popular and Folk.* New York: Crown, 3rd. ed., rev. and enlarged, 1985.

Horowitz, Helen Lefkowitz. *Alma Mater: Design and Experience in the Women's Colleges from Their Nineteenth-Century Beginnings to the 1930s.* New York: Knopf, 1984.

Schwarz, Judith. *"Yellow Clover:* Katharine Lee Bates and Katharine Coman." *Frontiers,* **IV,** no. 1, 1979.

Julia Ward Howe

Bristol, Frank Milton. *The Life of Chaplain McCabe.* New York: Fleming Revell, 1908.

Claghorn, Charles E. *Battle Hymn (The Story Behind the Battle Hymn of the Republic).* New York: Hymn Society of America, 1974, pp. 4–14.

Clifford, Deborah. *Mine Eyes Have Seen the Glory: A Biography of Julia Ward Howe.* Boston: Little, Brown, 1979.

Donald, David. *Charles Sumner and the Coming of the Civil War.* New York: Knopf, 1960.

Flexner, Eleanor. *Century of Struggle: The Woman's Rights Movement in the United States*. Harvard University Press, 1975.

Fuld, James J. *The Book of World Famous Music. Classical, Popular and Folk*. New York: Crown, 3rd. ed., rev. and enlarged, 1985.

Hall, Florence Howe. *The Story of the Battle Hymn of the Republic*. New York: Harper, 1916.

Howe, Julia Ward. *Reminiscences 1819–1899*. Boston: Houghton Mifflin, 1899.

Meltzer, Milton. *A Light in the Darkness: The Life of Samuel Gridley Howe*. New York: Crowell, 1964.

Oates, Stephen B. *To Purge This Land with Blood: A Biography of John Brown*. New York: Harper, 1970.

Richards, Laura E. and Elliott, Maude Howe. *Julia Ward Howe, 1819–1910* (2 vols.). First published 1925; reprinted by Norman S. Berg, 1970.

Schwartz, Harold. *Samuel Gridley Howe, Social Reformer 1801–1876*. Boston: Harvard University, 1965.

Snyder, Edward D. "The Biblical Background of the Battle Hymn." *New England Quarterly*, **24** (1951), 231–38.

Stutler, Boyd B. *Glory, Glory, Hallelujah!: The Story of John Brown's Body and Battle Hymn of the Republic*. Cincinnati: C.J. Krehbiel, 1960.

Thomas, Lately. *Sam Ward, King of the Lobby*. Boston: Houghton Mifflin, 1965.

Wilson, Edmund. *Patriotic Gore*. New York: Oxford, 1962.

Helen Hunt Jackson

Banning, Evelyn I. *Helen Hunt Jackson*. New York: Vanguard, 1973.

Edelstein, Tilden G. *Strange Enthusiasm: A Life of Thomas Wentworth Higginson*. New Haven: Yale, 1968.

Gruver, Rebecca Brooks. *An American History* (2 vols.). Reading MA: Addison-Wesley, 1972.

Higginson, Thomas W. *Contemporaries*. Boston: First published 1899; reprinted by Literature House, 1970.

James, George Wharton. *Through Ramona's Country*. Boston: Little, Brown, 1909.

Odell, Ruth. *Helen Hunt Jackson*. New York: D. Appleton-Century, 1939.

Sewell, Richard B. *The Life of Emily Dickinson* (2 vols.). New York: Farrar, Straus and Giroux, 1974.

Wells, Anna Mary. *Dear Preceptor,: The Life and Times of Thomas Wentworth Higginson*. Boston: Houghton Mifflin, 1963.

Emma Lazarus

Allen, Frederick. "Saving the Statue." *American Heritage*, **35**, no. 4, 1984, 97–109.

Allen, Leslie. *Liberty: The Statue and the American Dream.* New York: The Statue of Liberty/Ellis Island Foundation, 1985.

Angoff, Charles. *Emma Lazarus: Poet, Jewish Activist, Pioneer Zionist.* Jewish Historical Society of New York, pub. no. 3, 1979.

The Art Amateur, **X,** Jan. 1884. Supp. 41–48.

The Art Amateur, **X,** Feb. 1884, 58.

Baym, Max I. "Emma Lazarus and Emerson." *Publications of the American Jewish Historical Society*, **XXXVIII** (1949), 261–87.

Gilder, Rodman. *Statue of Liberty Enlightening the World.* New York: New York Trust Co., 1943.

"Growth of a Nation." *Time*, **126,** no. 2, 1985 history section, 34–35.

Higham, John. *Send These to Me.* Baltimore: Johns Hopkins, rev. ed., 1984.

"Immigration." *The Wilson Quarterly*, **VII,** no. 1, 1983, 100–131.

Jacob, H.E. *The World of Emma Lazarus.* New York: Shocken, 1949.

Lazarus, Josephine. *Poems of Emma Lazarus.* Boston: Houghton Mifflin, 1889.

"Liberty Stands on Her Words." *Ms.*, Gazette News, Aug. 1977.

Mordell, Albert. "Some Final Words on Emma Lazarus." Publications of the American Jewish Historical Society, **XXXIX** (1950), 324–25.

"Passing on the Torch." *Time*, **124,** no. 2, 1984, special advertising supplement, 37–52.

Pauli, Hertha. "The Statue of Liberty Finds Its Poet." *Commentary*, **1,** 1945–46, 56–64.

Russell, John A. "A Face that Really Launched 1,000 Ships — and Many More." *Smithsonian*, **15,** no. 4, 1984, 47–55.

Schappes, Morris U., ed. *The Letters of Emma Lazarus.* New York: New York Public Library, 1949.

Vogel, Dan. *Emma Lazarus*, Boston: G.K. Hall, 1980.

Mary Lyon

Conway, Jill Kerr. "The 19th Century Origins of Education for Women." *Middlebury College Magazine*, Winter 1983, 8–14.

Cremin, Lawrence A. *American Education: The National Experience 1783–1876.* New York: Harper, 1980.

Fisk, Fidelia. *Recollections of Mary Lyon, with Selections from Her Instructions to the Pupils in Mount Holyoke Female Seminary.* Boston: American Tract Society, 1866.

Frothingham, Paul Revere. *Edward Everett: Orator and Statesman*. First published 1925; reprinted by Kennikat, 1971.

Goodsell, Willystine. *Pioneers of Women's Education in the United States: Emma Willard, Catherine Beecher, Mary Lyon*. New York: McGraw Hill, 1931.

Green, Elizabeth Alden. *Mary Lyon and Mount Holyoke: Opening the Gates*. Hanover: University Press of New England, 1979.

Hitchcock, Edward. *The Power of Christian Benevolence Illustrated in the Life and Letters of Mary Lyon*. Philadelphia: Hopkins, Bridgman, 1852.

Lansing, Marion Florence, ed. *Mary Lyon Through Her Letters*. Boston: Books, Inc., 1937.

Pierce, B.K. "Mary Lyon and Her Seminary." *National Repository*, Feb. 1877, 12–28.

Harriet Beecher Stowe

Ammons, Elizabeth. *Critical Essays of Harriet Beecher Stowe*. Boston: G.K. Hall, 1980.

Ashton, Jean W. *Harriet Beecher Stowe: A Reference Guide*. Boston: G.K. Hall, 1977.

Gossett, Thomas F. *Uncle Tom's Cabin and American Culture*. Dallas: Southern Methodist University, 1985.

Dumond, Dwight L. *Antislavery: The Crusade for Freedom in America*. Ann Arbor MI: University of Michigan, 1961.

Hildreth, Margaret Holbrook. *Harriet Beecher Stowe: A Bibliography*. Hamden CT: Shoe String, 1976.

Kirkham, E. Bruce. *The Building of Uncle Tom's Cabin*. Knoxville: University of Tennessee, 1977.

Nye, Russel B. *William Lloyd Garrison and the Humanitarian Reformers*. Boston: Little, Brown, 1955.

Reynolds, Moira D. *Uncle Tom's Cabin and Mid-Nineteenth Century United States: Pen and Conscience:* Jefferson NC: McFarland, 1985.

Rugoff, Milton. *The Beechers: An American Family in the Nineteenth Century*. New York: Harper and Row, 1981.

Sklar, Kathryn Kish. *Catherine Beecher: A Study in Domesticity*. New Haven: Yale University, 1973.

Stowe, Charles E. *Life of Harriet Beecher Stowe*. Boston: Houghton Mifflin, 1889.

Weld, Theodore D. *American Slavery As It Is: Testimony of A Thousand Witnesses*. First published 1839; reprinted by Arno, 1969.

Wilson, Forrest. *Crusader in Crinoline: The Life of Harriet Beecher Stowe*. Philadelphia: Lippincott, 1941.

Emma Hart Willard

Bartlett, Ellen Strong. "Emma Willard, a Pioneer of Education for Women." *New England Magazine,* Jan. 1902, 555–76.

Cubberley, Elwood P. *Public Education in the United States: A Study and Interpretation of American Educational History.* Boston: Houghton Mifflin, 1919.

Elsbree, Willard S. *The American Teacher.* First published 1939; reprinted by Greenwood, 1970.

Johnson, Clifton. *Old-Time Schools and Schoolbooks.* First published 1904; reprinted by Dover, 1963.

Koestle, Carl F. *Pillars of the Republic: Common Schools and American Society 1780–1860.* New York: Hill and Wang, 1983.

Lord, John. *The Life of Emma Willard.* New York: D. Appleton, 1873.

Lutz, Alma. *Emma Willard, Pioneer Educator of American Women,* First published 1964; reprinted by Greenwood, 1983.

Moorefield, Story. "One Woman's Fight." *American Education,* Nov. 1974, 80–1.

Phelps, Stephen. "The Indomitable Emma Willard." *Conservationist,* March–April, 1970, 17–19.

Stanton, Elizabeth Cady. *Eighty Years and More: Reminiscences 1815–1897.* First published 1898; reprinted by Shocken, 1971.

Tyler, Alice Felt. *Freedom's Ferment: Phases of American Social History to 1860.* Minneapolis: University of Minnesota, 1944.

Woody, Thomas. *A History of Women's Education in the United States.* First published 1929; reprinted by Octagon, 1974.

Index

Photo pages appear in **bold.**